TWO FRENCHMEN

By the same author

PERSONALITY IN POLITICS (1939)

THE DEMOCRATIC IDEAL IN FRANCE AND ENGLAND (1940)

DEMOCRACY IN FRANCE; THE THIRD REPUBLIC (1946)

THE BABEUF PLOT (1947)

EQUALITY (1949)

ENGLAND IN THE NINETEENTH CENTURY (1950)

TWO FRENCHMEN

Pierre Laval
and
Charles de Gaulle

by

DAVID THOMSON

Senior Tutor of Sidney Sussex College,
Cambridge

LONDON
THE CRESSET PRESS
MCMLI

TO MY WIFE

First published in 1951 by the Cresset Press, Ltd.,
11, Fitzroy Square, London, W.1
and printed in Great Britain at The Chapel River
Press, Andover, Hants
12.50

PREFACE

THE TWO FRENCHMEN whose lives I have here described have both played a decisive part in the modern development of France. No up-to-date English account of their lives or of their importance so far exists. It is hoped that the two studies which follow will, to some extent, explain these enigmatic figures to English readers. Various materials which have become available during the last five years have made a more rounded study of them possible; although it is not pretended that these studies are more than an interim judgment on two controversial personalities, one of whom from his grave still stirs ugly passions in the hearts of so many Frenchmen, the other of whom is still a mighty imponderable in the course of French politics. Definitive judgment must await the wisdom of greater hindsight than is yet possible. But at a time when the future of the British Commonwealth and the French Union are so intimately bound up together, and when British understanding of what has happened in France is more than ever important, it may be of value to reach even provisional judgments about the forces at work.

It is hoped, too, that the juxtaposition of these two studies may in itself help to throw light on some of the *nuances* of French politics, which are the most intangible of all for the non-Frenchman to grasp, or even to perceive. Pierre Laval had held many high ministerial offices in France before Charles de Gaulle had even been heard of in public life. The crisis of

1940 threw them into leadership of opposite camps, and it might seem that thenceforward they had nothing in common. But in fact their fates were closely intertwined. Between them they have dominated the last decade of French affairs, and it is more than possible that the future historian of France will regard them as having made complementary responses to the challenge of national defeat. The historian may even come to discern in their complete refusal to see that their responses were complementary the greatest tragedy of the defeat and the most potent factor in the making of the Fourth Republic. To a remarkable degree Frenchmen tend to view each other politically in the way they do because of what Laval and de Gaulle did during the decade between 1940 and 1950; and the execution of Laval, upon which de Gaulle insisted, was in itself no escape from the dilemma.

Although the words uttered by each man are of importance, I have tried to treat actions as of more importance than words in reaching an interpretation of the men. I have in each case attempted to get behind the caricatures which have so far been accepted as substitutes for portraits.

I have not attempted to provide a comprehensive bibliography, which would inevitably be almost immediately out of date; but I have indicated in footnotes the main sources of material. It is hoped that the authors and publishers of all these works will regard this indication as carrying with it an acknowledgement of my debt of gratitude to them. I wish particularly to acknowledge the kindness of the following authors and publishers who have given permission to quote from the publications mentioned:

Cassell & Co., Ltd.—Winston S. Churchill, *Their Finest Hour*, Volume II of *The Second World War*. Contact Publications, Ltd.—D. M. Pickles, *France between the Republics*. Eyre & Spottiswoode, Ltd.—*The Private Diaries of Paul Baudouin*. The Falcon Press, Ltd.—*The Unpublished Diary of Pierre Laval*. Victor Gollancz, Ltd.—Admiral W. D. Leahy, *I Was There*; and Henry Torrès, *Pierre Laval*. Hamish Hamilton, Ltd.—D. W. Brogan, *The Development of Modern France, 1870–1939*; D. W. Brogan, *French Personalities and Problems*; and *The Goebbels Diaries*, edited by Louis Lochner. George G. Harrap & Co., Ltd.—Pierre Tissier, *I Worked with Laval*. William Heinemann, Ltd.—*Ciano's Diary*, 1939–1943. Hodder & Stoughton, Ltd. and Madame Bois—Élie-J. Bois, *Truth on the Tragedy of France*. Hutchinson & Co., Ltd.—Charles de Gaulle, *France and her Army*. Odham's Press, Ltd.—*Ciano's Diplomatic Papers*. Oxford University Press—*Speeches of General de Gaulle*.

I want also to record my thanks to the Editor of *The Spectator* and Dr. B. S. Townroe for permission to quote the passage on page 142, and to Mr. Norman Hunt for his great kindness in reading the proofs.

D. T.

CAMBRIDGE, *August* 1950.

Cassell & Co. Ltd.—Winston S. Churchill, *Their Finest Hour*, Volume II of *The Second World War*. [illegible] Publications, Ltd.—D. M. [illegible] [illegible] Eyre & Spottiswoode, Ltd.—*The* [illegible] *Pool* [illegible] The Falcon Press, Ltd.—[illegible] [illegible] Ltd.—[illegible] W. R. [illegible] and [illegible] Hamish Hamilton, Ltd.—D. W. Brogan, *The Development of* [illegible] D. W. Brogan, *French Personalities and Problems*, and *The* [illegible] Lewis [illegible] George G. Harrap & Co., Ltd.—[illegible] William Heinemann, Ltd.—[illegible] Hodder & Stoughton, Ltd.—[illegible] [illegible] & Co., Ltd.—[illegible] Oxford University Press [illegible]

I want also to record my thanks to [illegible] of [illegible] and Dr. E. [illegible]

[illegible]

[illegible] in reading the proofs.

D. T.

Cambridge, [illegible] 1950

CONTENTS

Pierre Laval

I have been accused of lacking ideals, doubtless because I always believed and still believe that foreign policy, though it must take into account some imponderables, should always be based on solid realities. Regimes follow one another in solemn procession, governments undergo revolutions, but geography remains invariable. We will be neighbours of Germany for ever.

(*Pierre Laval*)

Laval is a filthy Frenchman—the filthiest of all Frenchmen.

(*Count Ciano*)

Ce Laval—quel fumier! (*Marshal Pétain*)

THERE IS A dramatic unity about the life of Laval which it has become possible to appreciate only since his very dramatic death. There are even a coherence and a continuity in his ideas which are unexpected in one whose most conspicuous political habit was opportunism. He is the modern practitioner of political aims and political methods which have close links with the ideas of Georges Sorel, perhaps the only political thinker—apart from the veteran revolutionary, Auguste Blanqui—to whom Laval would have owed any debt or allegiance.

His *Diary*, which he wrote in the prison-cell at Fresnes while awaiting the foregone verdict of his "trial", and which his devoted daughter, Josée de Chambrun, smuggled out page by page, is the only book he ever wrote. It contains this significant remark: "Even the most casual examination of my political career will prove conclusively that never having sought popularity I never aspired to be a dictator."[1] If this remark is a good deal less than frank, in that it ignores his early rise to parliamentary power, and was part of his brilliant self-defence against the accusation of treason in 1945, it nevertheless points to one significant feature of his whole career. He became one of the least trusted and most bitterly detested men in the whole of France. The interlude of Vichy only brought to a climax a process which had been maturing throughout the entire period of his most active parliamentary career, during which he held eighteen ministerial offices and was three times Premier of France. Certainly no one, at least from 1930 onwards, could accuse Laval of courting popularity, or even of seeking to inspire trust. Like Walpole in eighteenth-century England, he was too apt to handle politics in the basest materialistic terms to attract enthusiasm in a country where political ideas wield almost an independent power over the minds of men. To understand this streak in his character and this strand in his mode of thought we must go back to his youthful enthusiasms and his early struggles for influence.

As he never forgot, and never allowed his associates to forget, he was essentially a son of Auvergne. He was born, on 28th June, 1883, at Chateldon in the northern part of that province. His father combined the jobs of café-proprietor, village butcher, and local postman, and was sufficiently well-to-do to own a few acres of vineyard and half a dozen horses. The

[1] *The Unpublished Diary of Pierre Laval* (1948), p. 69.

Auvergnats are notoriously some of the most hard-headed and canny of French peasants; and when they have made money elsewhere, whether by selling coal and wood and chestnuts or by other more distinguished but less reputable means, they return to their native Auvergne to live again the life of a peasant. So did Pierre, when he had collected a fortune by various devices which shall be later discussed, buy the medieval castle which dominates Chateldon and seek refuge there whenever his political fortunes made possible his prolonged absence from Paris.

He was a conventionally naughty choir-boy at the village church. He went to the village school, and when he had duly—at the age of twelve—passed with brilliance his *certificat d'études primaires*, his father took him away and made him drive the mail-coach in preparation for learning the trade and taking over the family business. But the determined and resourceful Pierre had other ambitions, and meant to continue his studies as soon as he could. He studied text-books whilst driving his horses, and at sixteen he persuaded his father to let him go to Paris to take his *baccalauréat* —the French equivalent of School Certificate. At first his interests lay in the natural sciences, and when he had successfully passed both parts of his examination he went to Lyons to study in the Faculty of Science. There he remained for a year, serving as *pion* or junior master in the *lycée* of Lyons to pay the costs of his board and lodging. And there his interests shifted from natural to social and political sciences. In the great industrial town he picked up extreme syndicalist views. He became familiar with the doctrines of Georges Sorel, whose ideas at the turn of the century were penetrating extremist Left-wing circles along with the kindred doctrines of Hubert Lagardelle. He propagated these ideas at debating societies and clubs in the working-class suburbs of Perrache and Les Brotteaux. When his contract at the *lycée* expired he moved on to a similar post at the college of Autun in Burgundy, and a year later to the big industrial town of Saint-Étienne, second in importance only to Lyons, in that part of France, for its powerful revolutionary traditions. Here he joined the Socialist Party, and supported the Blanquist section of the Revolutionary Central Committee. It was 1903, and the keen-minded, shrewd young man of twenty was caught up into that tide of syndicalist ideology and agitation which made the 1900's a decade of remarkable proletarian unrest in France.

After a year's conscript service in the Army, from which he was discharged because of his varicose veins, he resumed his work as a teacher. By 1907 he was working in the *Lycée Louis le Grand* in Paris. Here he finally abandoned natural science, and took up Law. But the short-lived flirtation—for it was little more—with study of the material sciences has some significance. Did it not fit him better to understand the political ideas of "technicians", like Sorel and Pareto? He tried to form a monitors' trade-union, in defiance of the prevailing official view that teachers, like other public servants, had no right to join the recently-created *Confédération Générale du Travail.* He gained only six other adherents, all of them at the same *lycée* as himself. Despite his gaining an interview with the Minister of Public Instruction, whom he talked into believing that his union represented 775 out of the

800 monitors employed in Paris, his project came to nothing.[1] At the age of twenty-five he began his career at the Bar. But his resolve was to use it as the *entrée* to politics, not as a profession. He became secretary to Ernest Lafont, also a disciple of Lagardelle and Sorel and lawyer for the *Confédération Générale du Travail*. His job was to defend trade-unionists against prosecutions for the many technical misdemeanours of trade-unions in those early days. "Over these juridical controversies", Henry Torrès has written, "floated the lofty shadow of Blanqui, the great insurrectionist, for Laval was becoming more and more of a Blanquist."[2] The day-to-day incidents of the workers' struggle for improvement of their material lot, and the constant issues of conflict between syndicalist bodies and the State, chimed in well with the doctrines he had first imbibed at Lyons and Saint-Étienne. Thus his political apprenticeship was spent in the three greatest centres of industrial unrest and of revolutionary fanaticism. Meanwhile he married the daughter of Dr. Claussat, formerly mayor of Chateldon, member of the General Council of the *département*, and deputy of the district. The country doctor was an advanced Republican and Radical, in the Clemenceau tradition.

In the capital he made the acquaintance of most of the extremist left-wingers of the time, including his legal colleague Jean Longuet. Longuet was born into the authentic revolutionary heritage, being a grandson

[1]Henry Torrès, *Pierre Laval* (1942), p. 15. He later liked to tell anecdotes of how he had paid for his own education by teaching, and thought it more to his credit than if he had held scholarships (cf. Pierre Tissier, *I Worked with Laval* (1941), p. 35).

[2]*Op. cit.*, p. 18.

of Karl Marx, the son of the Communard, and godson of Clemenceau. Longuet remained of some importance in Laval's later life. Pierre attended innumerable trade-union meetings and conferences, and won their hearts when he spectacularly secured the acquittal of one of their anarchist members, Manès. (Manès had been found by the police lying unconscious in a pool of blood, near a sabotaged telegraph line, with a pair of wire-cutters in his hand.) His trade-unionist clientèle grew steadily. Despite an unsuccessful stand as candidate for the by-election at Boulogne-sur-Seine in 1911, he laid plans to become a deputy in the general elections of 1914. He canvassed and nursed the tough working-class industrial constituency of Aubervilliers, in the north-east suburbs of Paris. On the second ballot he was returned with a solid majority. He was the youngest socialist deputy in the new Chamber of 1914; and entered it just in time for his parliamentary position to secure his immunity from war service. His name was on the famous *Carnet B*, the list of anarchists and other suspects prepared by the *Sûreté Générale* for immediate arrest in the event of mobilization. He was paradoxically saved from arrest by the murder of Jean Jaurès, because Malvy, the Minister of the Interior, was loath to provoke further the workers who were already outraged by the shooting of their great leader. He tore up the list, and Laval was, equally paradoxically, appointed to membership of the Army Committee of the Chamber. His political career had begun at last, at the age of thirty-one and in the most momentous of circumstances. The first World War confronted all French socialists with the dilemma whether they should be true to their internationalist principles or to the patriotic duty to support their country.

On this issue the French socialists and trade unionists split. The majority of each supported the policy indicated by the dead Jean Jaurès, and abandoned the pacifist policy of the Second International for the duration of the war. This majority section included most of the great names of French socialism —Jules Guesde, Albert Thomas, Léon Blum, Léon Jouhaux, even Édouard Vaillant the Communard and Gustave Hervé the "pacifist". Laval found himself with Jean Longuet in the minority, in opposition to the Government and urging the restoration of contact with the German socialists to shorten the war and prepare for the peace. On 4th August Jaurès was buried, and that afternoon the majority of the socialists in the Chamber voted for war-credits and other measures for the prosecution of the war. Three weeks later the Prime Minister, René Viviani, enlarged his ministry to include three of their leaders—Jules Guesde, Albert Thomas and Marcel Sembat. The minority faction kept up an energetic campaign of propaganda against the war, bitterly denouncing their former colleagues whom they regarded as traitors to the cause of the International. In September 1915 the anti-war parties of the International met on neutral Swiss soil at Zimmerwald. They issued the famous "Zimmerwald Manifesto" which denounced the war as "the outcome of imperialism" and urged peace without annexations or indemnities. Lenin was there representing the Russian party; so were two of Laval's extremist trade-unionist friends, Merrheim and Bourderon. Back in Paris Longuet, Laval and their colleagues were busy supporting Trotsky, who was publishing a little Russian journal *Nash Slovo*, and creating the new Committee for the Re-establishment of International Relations. The major result of Zimmerwald was the eventual establishment of the Third (Communist) International, under the inspiration and guidance of Lenin and Trotsky. But that came only in 1917, and meanwhile the fragmentary groups, which were later to come together in this more permanent form, were busy spreading pacifist and defeatist propaganda, exploiting war-weariness and war-grievances in the belligerent countries, working through war-factories and workshops, and even within the armed forces. Support came from the Haute-Vienne, Isère and Seine, where the revolutionary tradition was most lively. It succeeded, to the extent that in France in 1917 there were strikes and mutinies and a powerful wave of defeatist feeling. News-sheets like the *Bonnet Rouge* and *La Vérité*, run by a troupe of shady and scurrilous journalists, were the chief press-organs of the movement. Laval seems to have been well in with the promoters and authors of these papers. Under Aristide Briand, who in October, 1915, succeeded Viviani as Prime Minister, they went on sapping France's will to sustain the war. When Briand fell, in March, 1917, Ribot and Painlevé, in rapid succession, equally failed to check either German successes or the decline of public morale on the home front. Between August, 1914, and February, 1917, one French soldier had died every minute. This is the real basis of the pacifist forces in French life which Laval came to represent.

At last, in November, 1917, Georges Clemenceau

took over with the simple policy of "je fais la guerre". For Laval and all his associates the time of reckoning had come. The paw of "The Tiger" was raised to strike where his more lamb-like predecessors had hesitated to move. All the socialists regarded him as their greatest enemy. Much that he did was harsh and much was unjust. He acted on the doctrine of emergency knowing no compromise: the Bolshevik Revolution was at that very moment breaking out in Russia.

The Bolshevik Revolution had startling and profound repercussions in France. Hostility to the Tsarist regime was traditional on the left; and the tactics adopted by Lenin seemed to be bearing a rich harvest. As Professor Denis Brogan has put it, "The French workers, who had been told about revolutions ever since 1871, who had been fed with violent words, taught to await the great day when the rifle and the barricade would replace the ballot box and the Parliament, had now before their dazzled eyes the spectacle of the great day coming. What had been, for over a generation, mere rhetoric in Paris had become reality in St. Petersburg. . . . What had been done in the capital of the Tsars could and should be done in the capital of the Revolution."[1] In short, the old smouldering embers of revolutionary fanaticism were fanned into a bright glow by the cold wind from the steppes, at the very moment when the fortunes of French defence in Europe seemed to be at their lowest ebb. It was for France the greatest crisis of the whole war, calling for supreme effort if national defeat was to be avoided. All parties, in the patriotic and in the revolutionary camps alike, realized that it was the

[1]D. W. Brogan: *The Development of Modern France*, 1870–1939 (1940), p. 532.

climacteric. But in the revolutionary camp there was a new-born confidence: and in 1918 it could be said that "the events in Russia, represented to the French proletariat as a successful application of Socialism, have made them so fanatical that all argument is impossible."[1]

It must be noted that these great issues had split the French revolutionary tradition itself, even the most extremist and violent wing of that tradition, the Blanquist. Veteran *Communards* like Édouard Vaillant, who to many embodied the tradition of Blanquism, supported the war wholeheartedly and with habitual fanaticism: whereas men like Longuet and Laval, who could claim equally to be disciples of Blanqui, opposed it. Was it perhaps that the urge to violence could find adequate expression in either course? What seems true, however, is that it was Longuet and Laval who, by 1918, were more in tune with the majority of the rank-and-file trade unionists and socialists than were the older and more distinguished leaders. It was all the greater a dilemma for them when their arch-enemy Clemenceau gained power. Already Painlevé had arrested the leaders of the *Bonnet Rouge* and its like. A few notorious characters, most notably Mata Hari, were shot or found dead. Malvy, who had held the Ministry of the Interior continuously from 1914 until 1917, was charged before the Senate with high treason, and his trial brought to light some of the more unsavoury crevices of French political life, such as the Governmental (and later the German) subsidies paid to the *Bonnet Rouge*. Even Joseph Caillaux was arrested, and has never since

[1] Quoted, *ibid.*, p. 534.

ceased protesting against the injustice.[1] It was indeed a cleansing of the parliamentary stables: but it was nearly all necessary, if France was to win the war.

And Laval? Malvy had done him many a good turn in the past. He spoke in the Chamber of Deputies in support of Malvy; he contrived to become a member of the parliamentary committee which was appointed to investigate the charges brought against Malvy. The committee prepared a confidential report to be presented to the Chamber for debate on 28th November, 1917. On 27th November the report appeared very fully in one of the big Paris newspapers. It was learned that Laval, on 26th, had slipped a copy of the secret report into his overcoat-pocket from which it had dropped to the floor where a reporter had picked it up. Was it accident, or merely an ingenious way of delivering goods which had been offered for sale and generously paid for? Henry Torrès, who describes the incident in some detail, uses it as the basis of his charge that Laval henceforth served as an informer for Georges Mandel, right-hand man of Clemenceau. According to M. Torrès, Mandel was resolved that only those in the anti-patriotic conspiracy would escape punishment who would at once enter his service; and he struck a bargain whereby Laval escaped the purge and imprisonment in return for acting as government agent in the Chamber and as government-informer in the socialist ranks. His task was to nurture doubts, create anxiety, precipitate hopeless attempts or preach moderation and compromise.[2] The thesis is, of course, that to save his own

[1]Cf. Joseph Caillaux, *Mes Mémoires, III: Clairvoyance et force d'âme dans les épreuves*, 1912–1930 (1947).

[2]*Op. cit.*, Chapter III, *passim.*

skin Laval now betrayed all those with whom he had worked for nearly twenty years; that these events mark the "conversion" of the revolutionary socialist into the power-lusting politician of the right, slyly seizing any and every opportunity for his own advancement and gain, without trace of scruple or conscience; and that he would now import into his handling of high ministerial office the shabby, squalid tactics of the conspirator, his purpose guided by no other cause but himself. It is an ingenious theory, including an explanation of the fact that Laval did retain contacts with his old trade unionist and socialist companions and with men like Caillaux and his friends. It serves as a plausible prelude to the final "treachery" of the years after 1940. Yet it is not entirely convincing. Against it are recollections of the similar charges of treachery brought against Blanqui himself; the readiness of Torrès who knew Laval well, writing in the stress of war-time from New York, to see him as the diabolical embodiment of treason; and several awkward facts which shall later be considered. It emphasizes, however, the degree of mistrust which Laval, by his sly methods and ambiguous behaviour even before 1940, inspired in so many men who knew him. He became a character of whom nothing was too bad to be believed, the very lowest creature in the scale of human morality. It is a picture so black as to challenge doubts. And the fact that fifty of the socialist minority movement, including Laval, opposed ratification of the Treaty of Versailles with Germany in 1919, is explained a little too glibly by the remark that "For the occasion Mandel gave Laval a free hand."[1]

[1] *Op. cit.*, p. 42.

Laval's own version of his early days as a revolutionary socialist and of his relations with the Socialist and Communist Parties is expressed in the letter which he wrote, from his prison at Fresnes, in September, 1945, to the presiding judge of his trial.

> I might add that as long as I belonged to the Socialist Party I accepted its rules of discipline. Specifically in 1917 I declined to participate in the Clemenceau Ministry as Under-Secretary of the Interior. I refused Clemenceau's proposal because he had asked me to offer to the Socialist Party a large measure of participation in his government, and the party turned down the proposal.
>
> In 1919 I was not in agreement with my Socialist comrades. Nevertheless, because I was elected to office by them in 1914, I preferred to stand by my political friends and run on a party label which had no chance of being accepted, rather than agree to the offer which had been made to me to head the national block which was overwhelmingly successful at the elections.
>
> The truth is that I left the Socialist Party at the end of 1920 of my own free will. I resigned when the party split into the Socialist and Communist parties. . . .
>
> I should like to say at once that I have retained a memory of my youth as a militant member of the extreme Left not only because it was the time of my youth, but because, in those days, I was surrounded by an enthusiasm, an impartiality, a generosity which I never again found in any environment. This youth of mine left an indelible impression upon me: a love of peace and a love and respect for the workers, for the little people of the world, and for true liberty.[1]

There is, indeed, a remarkably strong case for Laval's consistency of outlook. He had, both before and during the war, adopted an attitude of materialistic realism, of pacifism in the face of nationalistic wars, of resistance to all that meant material loss and

[1] *The Unpublished Diary of Pierre Laval,* pp. 18f.

suffering to the mass of the peasants and workers. To all who hold that such beliefs are, in themselves, treasonable, fallacious, dangerous, revolutionary—and clearly these beliefs deserve all such epithets in the eyes of the French patriot—the speeches and conduct of Laval are inevitably evil. But to say this is merely to echo the reception given to every revolutionary socialistic doctrine by large sections of more traditionalist opinion from the time of the French Revolution onwards. So violent a reaction nearly always brings with it imputations against the sincerity and honesty of the man who holds such doctrines, and no personal immorality becomes too great to be imputed to him. The legend of Gracchus Babeuf, so perversely and unwittingly fostered by opponents of his views throughout the whole nineteenth century, is typical of what happens.[1] But it must be noted that Laval at least held these doctrines when it would surely have paid him better, and advanced his career faster, to have held the contrary; and that he did not renounce them either in 1919 when he could safely have done so in the wave of nationalism which swept the country after the armistice, or in the early 1920's when he might still have sought more rapid political advancement by turning his coat. He was in fact defeated in the elections of 1919, but retained his close connections with the trade-union movement, the more extreme socialists and the Parisian industrial workers. At the Conference of Tours in 1920 Communists split from Socialists. In the winter of 1920–21 the Government charged the C.G.T. with unlawful political agitation and asked the courts to dissolve it.

[1]Cf. D. Thomson, *The Babeuf Plot* (1947), Chapter III.

Along with Paul-Boncour, Laval acted as one of its defence counsels, and although the court ordered the dissolution of the C.G.T. the order was never acted upon. Paul-Boncour writes:

> At the outset Maître Laval had figured amongst the extremists of the Socialist Party. The Communists had even been able to believe that he might win over to them the mayors of the Paris suburbs, who had for the most part joined them and amongst whom he had many friends—and many of them for long remained friendly with him. For this crafty man had a talent for keeping active friendships and real support even in those quarters most opposed to the policy that he had adopted. With a skill which was typical of him he did not go over to communism; but he profited from the split to carry out a manœuvre which is always difficult enough to do without fuss, of leaving the Socialist Party, "not wanting to choose", as he put it, "between the two sides of a schism which he deplored!" . . . He was always on the best of terms with the C.G.T. and with Jouhaux, for whom he acted as personal counsel.[1]

This seems to have been the first clear example of his adopting a strategy which he was to employ over and over again in his political career, and which he tried to import into the conduct of international affairs in the 1930's. To a large extent he succeeded in using it during the period of the Vichy Governments between 1940 and 1944. It was the old principle of the *tertius gaudens*, adopted and adapted with great subtlety, skill and success to parliamentary politics. It rested on the mechanical principle that in any balance of power, as in a see-saw, it is the man who stands in the very middle who can manipulate the balance. To the mind of Laval it clearly meant

[1] J. Paul-Boncour, *Entre deux Guerres, II: Les Lendemains de la Victoire, 1919–1934* (1945), p. 76.

political realism—the practice of the doctrine that any politician must regard it as a good thing for himself to wield power, and the assumption that material gains for himself, his party or his country which could thus be won by adroit manœuvre and manipulation of a balance of power without the use of violence were gains cheaply won, and therefore the greatest gains of all. It was a strategy instinctively attractive to one with the sly peasant mentality of the political Auvergnat, impatient with the lofty and airy idealistic policies vaunted by so many politicians of other parties, and convinced that the material interests of the French people demanded a policy designed to augment their relative decline in military power by such resources of diplomatic craft and guile. Viewed in this light, Laval's career from 1920 until his death fits into a uniform pattern. And to say this is not to minimize his readiness to use such a policy for his own material profits, no less than for the benefit of national interests as he conceived them. It is, after all, a strategy (or perhaps only a stratagem) of which his much more distinguished predecessors, including a Cardinal of the Catholic Church such as Richelieu, had not been entirely innocent.

But it is a mode of conduct which in no way lends itself to glorious exploits. It involves constant calculation of the main chance and of the precise balance of forces at work, since any sudden and unforeseen tipping of the balance may easily unseat the man who is in the middle. It leads into the somewhat dusky by-ways of incessant manœuvre, of subtle intrigue and compromise, of shady "understandings" and hasty readjustments. This is a realm where Laval, by temperament and talents, was peculiarly happy and thoroughly at home: and with long practice his mind seems to have become almost incapable of comprehending any other sort of political life. He found with solid satisfaction that his methods—if patiently and tirelessly enough used—not only brought great profit and recurrent periods of great power to himself, but were capable of serving France in her moments of upheaval. It was a choice of methods which proved particularly suitable to the parliamentary system of the Third Republic, with its multitude of political parties and its frequent ministerial crises. It was Laval's ignorance and misunderstanding of the international scene after 1930 which brought to disaster his efforts to transfer the same technique of power to foreign affairs, and it was his incomprehension of the very nature of Nazism which made his policy inappropriate to Europe after 1933. After the defeat of France in 1940, seeing yet another chance to use the same devices to salvage the fortunes of himself and of France, he clutched at power once more under the aegis of Marshal Pétain. It was the most desperate and dangerous gamble of his whole life: and it cost him his life in the end.

It seems that the first opportunity to experiment with this technique came after the split between Socialists and Communists in 1920: and the possibility of doing so was doubtless a strong temptation to try. He and Jean Longuet, almost alone amongst the old minority group, refused to go over to the Communists. The Socialists still included many of his old friends. He was admirably placed for keeping in touch with both camps. He is reported to have admitted that he thought, for a while, of going into business, but after long deliberations with his wife he decided to stay a lawyer, but to leave the Socialist Party. As he insisted in his *Diary*, he left it of his own volition and was not ejected. He called himself, in his campaigning posters, an "independent socialist". Bitter attacks on him by the Communists served only to rally right-wing opinion to him. In 1923 he was elected mayor of Aubervilliers, and the next year he again became a deputy. Jean Longuet was still his friend and collaborator, though he was defeated in the 1924 elections.

Laval, in the Chamber, belonged to the *Cartel des Gauches*, which supported a ministry composed mainly of Radicals, led by Édouard Herriot. He backed the amnesty which the Chamber granted to Caillaux, and spoke in support of Caillaux as he had supported Malvy some years before. Even if it be contended, as M. Torrès and others contend, that in both cases his purpose was selfish and opportunist, at least it must be admitted that he had the courage of his lack of convictions. Certainly a useful alliance was formed between the two men from that moment, because when, in April, 1925, Herriot fell and Painlevé formed a new ministry, it included both Caillaux as Minister of Finance and Laval as Minister of Public Works: but both were out of office again six months later, when Painlevé reshuffled his cabinet. A month after that, when Briand formed his eighth ministry, he made Laval Under-Secretary of State in charge of press relations. A few months later he was promoted to the Ministry of Justice under the same Premier; and it was normal for the Minister of Justice to serve also as Vice-President of the Council of Ministers. Laval had at last attained high office, and had won recognition from a succession of the political leaders as one of the *ministrables*, a man to be considered for cabinet posts in any parliamentary reshuffle of the left and centre parties. That is the hardest step in a rising politician's career.

It is clear that he could not have attained this status so quickly—at the age of forty-three—had he not detached himself from the Communist and Socialist Parties in 1920. It had been Socialist policy to hold aloof from official participation in any of the ministries in which they would not have a preponderant voice. The Communists, of course, were entirely excluded from office. But whilst keeping unattached to either of the party machines, it was necessary for the ambitious politician to keep very closely in touch with the electorate on which his fate depended. It was in this work that Laval excelled. His lack of membership of either of the official parties became an advantage. He could disagree and disobey with impunity any party decision on policy and strategy, and could exploit electoral discontent with the shortcomings and mistakes of both parties. He was able, in the cabinet crisis of June, 1926, to play a considerable part in the formation of the new Briand ministry, in which he again held the seals of the Minister of Justice. He succeeded again in bringing in his friend Caillaux as Vice-President of the Council of Ministers. But this arrangement lasted less than a month, and from the summer of 1926 until the spring of 1930, Laval retired into the wings of the political stage. He became a Senator in 1927 on the ticket of the "National

Republican Union", opposed to Socialist and Communist lists alike; and the Socialist list included the name of Jean Longuet. It is 1927, rather than 1920, which marks his real desertion from the left. It was to become a national joke that he had arranged to be born with a name which looked the same whether you were moving from left to right or from right to left. Laval got in on the first ballot for the department of the Seine. In the Senate he did not force himself to the front, partly because he knew how to wait and knew that his methods of personal lobbying would take time to install him in favour with the right in the Senate, after his desertion; and partly because he was all the time busy making his pile from his legal and semi-legal activities as a lawyer.

The sources and size of Laval's fortune have become legendary. It is certain that he made much of it in these years between 1920 and 1930, and that much of it came from his skill in keeping the affairs of wealthy clients out of the law-courts rather than by winning them in the law-courts. A man on the borderline between politics and law—again, a man in the middle of the see-saw—was in this first decade after the first war in a peculiarly strong position. Working in Paris he could attract some of the surplus wealth of the war profiteers and tax-evaders into his own coffers. Here is M. Torrès's version of how the basis of the fortune was laid.

> War profiteers desirous of keeping their profits; industrialists who had exaggerated their war damages and received undeserved indemnities; directors of corporations who diverted their firms' funds into their own pockets; bankers who gambled away their depositors' savings on baccarat tables; fraudulent brokers, food speculators,

> exploiters of the State, plunderers of public funds, and embezzlers—such were the men who supplied Pierre Laval with the foundations of his wealth.[1]

A counsel who knew personally so many members of the government and who had so many contacts with parliamentarians and civil servants was invaluable to such clients: and Laval had no scruple—indeed he probably persuaded himself that he was morally justified, if he ever considered the question of ethics at all—in rooking these rogues of some of their gains. After all, he was poor and had for long lived with the poor; and did not people admire those who robbed the rich for the benefit of the poor?

Certain it is that Laval eventually acquired a fortune large enough to buy an estate in Normandy, where he bred race-horses; to buy the castle at Chateldon and remodel and refurnish it, and to develop and speculate on the Chateldon springs, which Madame de Sévigné had preferred even to the springs of Vichy; to buy a series of newspapers, including the *Moniteur du Puy de Dôme* of Clermont-Ferrand, and the radio station of Radio-Lyons. But although his unscrupulous business acumen was great, and most of the business affairs which he handled brought him in ever-growing profits, it is probable that the extent of his private fortune has been exaggerated, as has most of the legend of Laval. It was alleged in 1945 that it amounted to fifty-seven or sixty million francs. The first charge brought against him in August, 1945, in the Act of Accusation, consisted of the statement that "The career of Laval before the war began in the parties of the Left, who

[1] *Op. cit.*, p. 73.

later repudiated him. He was several times a Minister, twice Prime Minister, and his personal fortune followed the course of his political fortune."[1]

After pointing out that neither of the first two statements in this charge was strictly correct, because he had left the Socialist Party in 1920 of his own free will, and had been Prime Minister not twice but three times, he went on, in his letter to the presiding judge of the court, to offer this explanation of the origins of his private wealth.

> I conclude from this section of the "accusation" that I am supposed to have amassed my capital from the vantage-point of my privileged position as a person holding office. I have always felt that a certain ease, a modicum of means, is a guarantee of political independence in a public officer. I have never heard it suggested that men in public life should not look after their personal affairs when these are not in conflict with the interests of the State. You may be surprised to learn that I was so scrupulous on this score that I consistently refused to appear in court against the State and against the City of Paris because I was a member of Parliament and a representative of the Department of the Seine. I shall surprise you less, as you are a veteran judge, when I tell you that my respect for the independence and dignity of the judicial office has consistently been so great that from the day when I was Keeper of the Seals (Minister of Justice) I never again appeared in court as a lawyer. . . . I defy anyone to show that at any time during the course of my public life I took advantage of any office to increase my estate.[2]

The statement is perhaps as significant for what it does not say as for what it does: but it seems likely that it was more his practice to use the fact of *having*

[1]*The Unpublished Diary of Pierre Laval,* Appendix III; *Le Procès Laval* (1946), p. 41.

[2]*Ibid.*, pp. 21f.

been in high office, and of knowing those who were in high office, to promote the interests of his clients and his own profits, than to abuse the power of office whilst he actually held it for his own monetary gains.

Pierre Tissier served as principal private secretary to Laval for some two years, while he was Minister of Labour, Minister of the Interior and Premier. He regards the origin of Laval's fortune as still inexplicable, and regards Torrès's explanation as insufficient. "It cannot be disputed", he writes, "that he is an exceedingly shrewd man of business and that—without any political element whatever coming into play—he made very large sums of money in his stock-farming operations as well as in the management and resale of his newspapers and his broadcasting station. But that is not enough to account for the huge improvement in his financial position. If we consider his extremely modest beginnings it is impossible to suppose that he never made use of his political position to further his personal interest."[1] The precise origins and sources of his private fortune were complex and remain obscure. But one factor in it was doubtless his own instinctive peasant thrift. On this all who knew him well are agreed: and M. Tissier sums it up well. "To Laval a sou remains a sou, and that whether it belongs to himself or to the State. He scrapes and stints on the salaries of the staffs of his papers as much as on payments out of the secret funds: we can be assured that he never paid for the most accommodating service more than it was worth. And then he is a past-master at promising a great deal and giving very little."[2]

* * * * *

[1]Pierre Tissier, *op. cit.*, pp. 45f.
[2]*Ibid.*, p. 36.

The secret of Laval's power in politics is less obscure than the secret of his private wealth. It appears obscure only to those who insist on regarding him as so incorrigibly villainous that it is impossible to explain how he could be so consistently returned by the industrial workers as Mayor of Aubervilliers and as Deputy or Senator. As he reminded the judge at his trial in 1945, "From 1914 until last year I was continuously elected Deputy and Mayor of Aubervilliers and an administrative decree was necessary to take this office away from me. This occurred a year ago, and thus a thirty-year relationship between the workers who are electors in this town and myself was brought to an end."[1] He was never an eloquent or impressive public speaker, and little of an orator. He was the only leading French politician who wrote practically nothing: his only writing is his *Diary*, written on the brink of the grave. His figure and features lent themselves to the most vicious and devastating caricature; in actual appearance he represented "the perfect type of the chestnut vendor or wine-seller in their Sunday best." Despite considerable attention to his dress, and especially to the spotlessness of his famous white silk tie, he seemed unable not to present a slovenly, untidy and unattractive appearance. Yet he was not, as those who knew him well attest (and contrary to what is commonly supposed) dirty and grubby. He paid a good deal of attention to cleanliness and attire. His famous grey lounge jacket, white tie and eternal cigarette were little different from the personal insignia of pipes, cigars, umbrellas and similar electioneering accoutrements of

[1]*The Unpublished Diary*, pp. 18f.

English and American politicians. It was his politics which were shabby, not his clothes.

He had, above all, remarkable charm. It is a point on which his most hostile critics are in agreement, even when they admit it grudgingly. M. Torrès writes, "He excels in discerning the secret stirrings of interest, envy, fear and hope behind the screen of faces. Though sometimes slow in finding words, he has a nimble wit. Despite his encyclopaedic ignorance and hesitant syntax, his calculated spontaneity, the studied simplicity and the unexpected flashes of colour in his expression make him both pleasant and dangerous in *tête-à-tête* conversations."[1] M. Tissier writes, "To anyone who only looks at Laval's exterior it may seem paradoxical to speak of his charm. Yet it was a very real thing. Personally, although I knew him well enough and knew just what his convictions were worth, I could never help succumbing to it. . . . But *a fortiori*, people who did not know Laval well were bound to be captured by his charm, by his power of convincing, his seeming good faith. Laval is the most admirable actor in the world. Furthermore, he has the gift of being always able to find the absolutely right word for everyone, and envelop him with a smile that makes it impossible to doubt his sincerity for a moment."[2] Mr. Alexander Werth wrote in 1937, "Pierre Laval is not impressive at first sight; and yet he has a personality which grows on you. He has an engaging smile and a charming voice which makes even newcomers perfectly comfortable; and even at the height of his power he never abandoned his old

[1]Torrès, *op. cit.*, p. 49.
[2]*Ibid.*, p. 40.

habits of camaraderie and tutoyage—a survival of his Socialist days."[1] That fine journalist and great patriot, Élie-J. Bois, wrote in 1941 this vivid description of Laval's mode of private address: "His face relaxed in that indescribable smile, peculiar to him, in which it is very difficult to discover how much is due to real pleasure and how much to pretended gaiety. Then in a regular monologue, whose originality I cannot reproduce, made up of grimaces, laughter, anecdotes, trenchant words, barbed shafts against some rival, intentional digressions and unexpected twists, M. Laval enlightened me—the word is his—about his position."[2]

This flair for captivating people, even in the most hostile and unfamiliar circumstances, was of inestimable value to him in his relations with other countries. When he visited the United States in 1931 it was reported to Briand that "M. Laval has conquered everyone by his frankness, though it is sometimes quite harsh, and by his graciousness: and the haughty austerity of Senator Borah himself yielded before his seductions. As for the American press, which is a *milieu* professionally tough and refractory, and with which M. Hoover has never succeeded in reaching an understanding, it is no exaggeration to say that it has literally been carried away. M. Laval has received, from reporters who jostled one another to hear him, veritable ovations. 'I thought I was at Aubervilliers,' he said to me with glee. The opinion generally expressed is that 'No man is better fitted to make himself understood in America.' "[3] There is

[1]Alexander Werth, *The Destiny of France* (1937), p. 103.
[2]Élie-J. Bois, *Truth on the Tragedy of France* (1941), p. 139.
[3]J. Baraduc, *Dans la Cellule de Pierre Laval* (1948), p. 68.

evidence—all the stronger for its being given so grudgingly—that he exerted this personal magnetism to some effect even over the Germans, and at a time of unusually strained relations between himself and the Nazis. Count Ciano records in his Diary for 19th December, 1942, that at the meeting in the gloomy forest of Gorlitz Laval made a deep personal impression. "Still," exclaimed Ciano, "how the Germans respond to the charm of the French! Even of this Frenchman. Except for Hitler, all the others were crowding around trying to talk to him, or to get close to him: it looked like the entrance of an erstwhile great lord into a circle of new-rich parvenus."[1]

These talents for personal conversation and group-persuasion were among his greatest political assets. He was one of the most plausible and persuasive people in the world. Knowing that this was his strength, he specialized in the kind of parliamentary business which is done in lobbies and corridors and in small committee-rooms. He was a man who worked in the wings, even when he was billed to hold the centre of the stage. He was an adept negotiator, so long as the negotiations could be conducted *à deux* or in very small groups: a specialist in wire-pulling and winning-over and "managing", whose repertoire ranged from agile argument through personal charm and flattery to veiled threats or even open blackmail. He was a highly skilled "technician" in politics, and as with so many pure "technicians" the end came to seem less important than the means. The most important thing was always to get his own way in the end.

And so it was that in the decade before the war

[1]*Ciano's Diary, 1939–1943* (1947), p. 537.

Pierre Laval became one of the leading parliamentarians of the Third Republic. A catalogue of his ministerial posts reveals this. From March to December, 1930, he was Minister of Labour under Tardieu; from January, 1931, until January, 1932, Prime Minister and Minister of the Interior; from January to February, 1932, Prime Minister and Minister of Foreign Affairs; then Minister of Labour again under Tardieu from February until June, 1932; Minister of Colonies under Doumergue from February until October, 1934; Minister of Foreign Affairs again from October, 1934, until June, 1935; Prime Minister again from June, 1935, until January, 1936, acting as his own Minister of Foreign Affairs. He was, for these years, a crucial force in both the domestic and foreign policy of France. Indeed his periods of greatest power were marked by moments of acute crisis in French affairs: the storm over the introduction of State insurance when he was Minister of Labour in 1930; the economic and financial crisis of 1931; the international crisis of the Abyssinian War in 1934-5. This enabled Laval to make a characteristic debating-point in his self-defence in 1945: "it would seem that whenever there was a critical period I was called upon to fill the breach."[1]

To the labours of ministerial office he brought precisely that political outlook and those methods of procedure which his earlier career would lead one to expect. Every question presented itself to him as a problem to be solved by parliamentary manoeuvre and through the manipulation of parliamentary opinion. In this respect he was completely a progeny of the Third Republic. On the theory of democracy which

[1] *The Unpublished Diary*, p. 40.

holds that ministries must be kept closely responsive to the majority of parliamentary opinion, Laval would appear to have been the most faithful and docile practitioner of parliamentary democracy. As M. Tissier puts it, "Briand used to swing the Chambers over to his policy, Laval lets his policy be shaped by the Chambers. . . . And so when he is faced with a problem he cannot cast about for its solution by asking himself what is the interest of the country or even, more simply, of a good administration. He gets one of his colleagues or one of his friends to explain it to him, and then he asks himself what will be the reaction of the parliamentary majority to each solution that can be presented to it. And he takes the solution likely to appeal to the greatest majority."[1] It meant that his conception of leadership was either non-existent or, at least, consisted in constantly placing himself at the head of whatever tide of parliamentary opinion he calculated to be the strongest. It was the policy of a weathercock, and it meant that the end always tended to be subordinated to the means. And yet, partly because of his skill in winning over hesitating floating-voters to the side which he conceived most likely to win the day, and partly because he so completely personified certain constant factors in French national life and opinion during these years, there is, as has been already suggested, a remarkable degree of consistency in his whole career. It is this paradox—of the weather-cock which to some extent could control the wind—which provides the fascination of the man.

The achievement of which he was proudest, and the only legislative accomplishment of any importance

[1]Tissier, *op. cit.*, pp. 41f.

which stands to his credit, was his successful carrying through of the social insurance legislation of 1930. When he first took over the Ministry of Labour he had to take charge of the debates in the Chamber on the bill concerning State insurance. The system had already been instituted under the auspices of Louis Loucheur, one of the big northern industrialists; but it at once became clear that it would need amendment and Laval had to pilot the draft bill of amendment through the National Assembly. The Chamber and the Senate were at cross-purposes—the perfect opening for Laval to bring to bear, on both, his genius for clever compromises and mutual concessions. M. Tissier, who was then Laval's private secretary and was engaged in the whole business, records that the texts actually voted upon by the two Chambers were not in the end identical, and it was "only by the employment of fraudulent 'errata' in the *Journal Officiel* that they were brought into agreement."[1] M. Tissier also records that the operation of the new schemes for State insurance was then caught up in a private war between two high officials in the Ministry, each of whom claimed to be the Director of State Insurance. They worked at cross-purposes and gave contradictory orders. Laval solved the problem by leaving the effective direction to one while giving the other the honorary, sinecure and illegal post of "Secretary-General to the Ministry". The task of bringing under a national scheme the thousands of small friendly societies in France was no easy matter, but Laval did it well.

As Minister of Labour he was also responsible for

[1]Tissier, *op. cit.*, p. 48.

settling labour disputes, a task which was of considerable importance at the time of the world economic slump and one for which his youthful connections with the workers and their trade unions (none of which he had willingly severed) stood him in good stead. Here again he was able to stand in the middle of the balance between workers and employers, knowing and understanding the outlook of both and serving as an invaluable go-between and arbitrator. He contrived, by a combination of showy concessions of principle and realistic concessions of material benefits, to end strikes of dockers and of textile workers. He would meet a hostile dockers' delegation at the Rue de Grenelle and "before five minutes had passed Laval, who began to 'tutoyer' each of the delegates, and called them all by their first names, had the whole deputation in his pocket".[1] It was the period of ministerial power of which he seems to have been most proud, and in his defence in 1945 he wrote, "As for my devotion to workers and to humble people I believe that I proved repeatedly by deeds that I always had their interest at heart. I should like to cite in particular my sponsorship of the law providing for family insurance and the law providing for social insurance, which I was able to have enacted despite the general hostility of Parliament. Perhaps I need not mention as well the innumerable conflicts in which workers were involved and which I was able to settle. I shall mention, just to give you a specific example, the great textile strike in the North in which 150,000 working men were involved."[2]

[1]Tissier, *op. cit.*, p. 54.

[2]*The Unpublished Diary*, p. 20. And cf. Torrès, *op. cit.*, p. 90.

When he became Prime Minister and Minister of the Interior he transplanted the same outlook and methods to the broader conduct of national domestic affairs, and had to wrestle with the consequences for France of the world economic crisis. He claimed to stand "above party", and indeed he contrived, as usual, to keep strong connections with both the Right and the Left. Because the Minister of the Interior controls the prefects and the whole centralized machinery of local administration in France, as well as the police and a share of the "secret funds", he is one of the most crucial and influential members of the Government. At times of general elections he was expected to "make the elections", in the sense of tipping the scale, through the prefects and electoral officers, in favour of the ministerial parties. It was a post entirely after Laval's heart. His system of "making elections", according to M. Tissier, was unusually adroit. He made the prefects support the candidates favoured by his majority in the Assembly, but at the same time he made payments from the secret funds to their opponents. He was thus sure to be on the winning side: he climbed on to both bandwaggons at once.

What he clearly enjoyed most was this control over so many of the levers of power by which public opinion could be manipulated. To keep his fingers on the pulse of public opinion, and especially of parliamentary opinion—for it was through this medium that all French ministries had to govern and sustain their own power—was work which peculiarly appealed to him. It gave him scope for his particular talents and guiles. And it was the one task in which he felt that he was bound to win. From this period dates his over-weening confidence in his own ability to get the better of anyone (and the best of both worlds) so long as he could induce his opponents to come within the ambit of personal or group negotiations. As we shall see he tried to bring foreign affairs—even Mussolini and Stalin and Hitler—within this same ambit.

It was whilst he was Prime Minister, in 1931, that there occurred the financial crisis in England which, in the *Diary* and documents published after his death, he claimed a central part in solving. The record of his behaviour on this occasion was indeed one of the most significant features of his adroit self-defence. Here is his account of what happened.

> In 1931, at the height of the great financial crisis, I received, in the middle of the night, at his urgent request, Sir Ronald Campbell, British Chargé d'Affaires in the absence of Lord Tyrell, the Ambassador. After hearing him I agreed, without reference to my Cabinet, for fear of an indiscretion which might affect British credit adversely, to make available the following morning from the French Treasury on a temporary loan basis the sum of three billions in gold. The coffers of the Bank of England were bare. Payments would have had to be suspended had it not been for the immediate and unstinted assistance of France. Sir Ronald Campbell thanked me with sincere emotion and said, taking my hands in his, 'M. le Président, I thank you. My country will never forget.'[1]

His daughter, in her introduction to the *Diary*, gives fuller details of the arrangement. According to her, Laval first offered half and suggested that the United States should be asked to subscribe the other half. "Personally", he added, "I don't believe that the United States will be in a position to agree to this, so

[1] *The Unpublished Diary*, pp. 26f.

come back tomorrow morning and if the United States do not agree to participate I will maintain my offer for the entire credit." The United States refused, and Laval fulfilled his promise of the full three billion francs.[1] Perhaps the most significant aspect of the whole affair, apart from its proof of a friendly response to Great Britain in time of her need, is the light it throws on Laval's extraordinary confidence in himself, and his supremacy over his colleagues in the ministry.

In June, 1935, he formed a ministry whose main task was to "save the franc". It was supposed to be a choice between deflation—which was a painful and unpopular process—and devaluation of the franc. Laval chose deflation, and appointed as his Minister of Finance M. Régnier, a radical senator who stood for this policy. He was granted plenary powers to deal with the economic crisis, and pundits said in the end that France needed neither deflation nor devaluation but simply "de-lavaluation". He cut by governmental decree the interest on government bonds, the rent of houses and mortgages, official salaries and pensions. He cut them by as much as ten per cent. He increased taxation. He took powers to fix by decree prices and profits in almost every branch of business in France. It was a merciless and wittingly unpopular policy, and yet much of French opinion preferred it to the risks of devaluation. By the end of October, 1935, Laval's government had issued no fewer than 500 decrees for "the defence of the franc": although some of these had so remote a connection with finance—such as the decree forbidding foreigners living in France to keep carrier-pigeons—that many began to suspect abuse

[1] *Ibid.*, pp. 10f. and Appendices I and II.

of the grant of emergency powers. Even so, his remedies proved only temporary. The French budgets soon reverted to their chronic habits of unbalance. But he did restore confidence in the franc for a time, and could claim that by his political courage he had stemmed a decline which, had inflation continued unchecked, might have cost France dear.[1]

In international affairs Laval was confronted with a series of vital issues: the death-throes of the Weimar Republic of Germany and the rise of Hitler; the problem of the Saar; the Abyssinian crisis and the imposition of League of Nations sanctions; the eternal problem of relations between Russia and the western Powers. They were, indeed, the events on which much of the future of Europe hung. But equally important, from the point of view of assessing his policy and his subsequent defence of his actions, are the issues which were settled while he was not in office: he was not in control of French policy at the moment when Hitler came into power in 1933, nor when Hitler occupied and remilitarized the Rhineland in 1936, nor when Hitler carried out his series of aggressions against Austria, Czechoslovakia and Poland from 1938 onwards. Whatever responsibility he may fairly share for events before the end of 1935, and whatever criticisms may be levied against the policy he urged from 1936 onwards, he cannot be justly saddled with any responsibility for the actual conduct of French foreign policy during the crucial years from 1936 onwards, when Hitler was gaining one strategic advantage after another in Europe. Because his accusers in 1945 overlooked this distinction, they gave

[1]On these events and their background, see Alexander Werth, *op. cit.*, Chapter IX.

him more than enough elbow-room to put forward a very powerful defence.

He inaugurated his control of foreign policy in 1931, when he was Prime Minister, by embarking on personal visits to Berlin and Washington. He was the first French Premier to visit either officially. Both visits were lavishly publicized, both at home and abroad. Germany was beset with mass unemployment and welcomed any hope of economic agreement with France. As a result of his visit a committee was set up "to examine the economic problems concerning the two nations without neglecting the interests of third nations". It ended by encouraging the investment of French capital in German industrics, but little else. When a month later Laval arrived in New York he announced that he had three questions to discuss with President Hoover: the gold standard, disarmament, and war-debts: but again little material result followed, and M. Herriot condemned this policy of "improvised trips and negotiations". Laval seems to have completely under-estimated the complexity and intractability of international relations. He assumed, with excessively cheerful self-confidence, that his familiar and well-tried methods of personal persuasion and lobbying could short-circuit the laborious and elaborate procedure of professional diplomacy. He tried to replace patient negotiation by hasty improvisation. Although his first excursions into foreign affairs won him wider international reputation and publicity, and were received complacently at home, he was too much of a realist not to have appreciated that the material gains, either for himself or his country, were extremely slender. This did not deter him from continuing the same method of direct and personal negotiation with the mighty dictators of Europe, when the stakes were even greater.

The years 1934-5 were dominated by the resurgence of German militant (and militarist) nationalism. Hitler was in power and had ostentatiously left the League of Nations. The policy of Louis Barthou, who preceded Laval as Minister of Foreign Affairs, was to establish fresh links with Russia. Russia was admitted to the League in September, 1934. Barthou had toured central and eastern Europe strengthening French ties with Germany's eastern neighbours. It was the minimum measure of reinsurance called for by the revival of German power. In October, 1934, he was assassinated at Marseilles, along with King Alexander of Yugoslavia. Laval seems to have already adhered in a general way to the policy urged by Fernand de Brinon and his Franco-German Committee (*Comité France-Allemagne*)[1], and had decided that France must seek understanding with Germany at any price. In December, 1934, de Brinon arranged a meeting between Laval and Ribbentrop in Paris; in January, 1935, the Saar was returned to Germany after a plebiscite held in accordance with the Treaty of Versailles. When, two months later, Hitler reintroduced conscription in violation of Versailles, Laval protested and lodged a formal complaint with the League of Nations. In May he signed the Franco-Soviet Pact of Mutual Assistance which Barthou had originally planned, and the next week took his

[1]Fernand de Brinon was a political journalist who combined this trade with managing large racing-stables and with dabbling in amateur diplomacy. Cf. his *France-Allemagne* (1934) for a full statement of his political ideas at this time.

daughter Josée to visit the Kremlin, stopping off at Warsaw on the way. On 15th May, 1935, he and Stalin issued a joint *communiqué* stating that "M. Stalin understands and fully approves of France's policy of national defence, intended to maintain her armed forces at the level demanded by security." On the way back he met Goering at Cracow and had a long *tête-à-tête* with him. Although no *communiqué* was issued after this meeting, it seemed all too probable that Laval was importing into the delicate intricacies of international power-politics the familiar techniques of the see-saw. To Mr. G. Ward Price he said that "one of his reasons" for signing the Pact between France and Russia was the fear that if France did not make such a pact, Germany might.[1] Even this motive was given some justification four years later when Hitler and Stalin did precisely this. The general impression left by these negotiations was that though Laval was formally continuing the policy inaugurated by Barthou he was acting with less earnestness and with one eye glancing over his shoulder at the possibility of similar pacts with the fascist dictators. It was a reversion to his favourite tactics of acting as the middle-man and the manipulator of the balance of power.

Meanwhile, he was pursuing an equally ambiguous policy with Mussolini. The staged incidents at Wal-Wal took place in December, 1934, and the next month Abyssinia appealed to the League. The same day Laval and Josée set off for Rome for three days' negotiations, which resulted in the agreement of 7th January, 1935. It offered Mussolini frontier modifications in Eritrea and Libya, an extension of the agree-

[1] G. Ward Price, *I Know these Dictators* (1937), p. 149.

ment of 1896 about Tunisia, and Italian participation in the Addis Ababa railway; and it seems probable that Laval in effect promised not to obstruct Italian predominance in Abyssinia. At the end of 1935, he admitted in the Chamber that "By waiving French rights I granted Italy the right to ask for concessions in all Ethiopia." Mussolini had remarked, "It is a pleasure to talk with him. I venture to believe that there is personal sympathy between us, because our tormented youths had something in common, because our experiences have been similar, because our similar evolution has led us away from a somewhat utopian universalism to profound and indestructible national realities." Mussolini, too, had been a disciple of Sorel and something of a syndicalist socialist. Laval is reported to have said, "If I have been so generous with Mussolini it is . . . because I need the friendship of Italy to reach an understanding with the Germans. And to achieve peace in Europe and in the world, an understanding with Germany is indispensable."[1]

In April, 1935, a three-power conference was held at Stresa, primarily to discuss German conscription and resurgence and to reassert the principles of Locarno. Laval and Flandin attended it for France. Italy joined with France and Britain in forming a "Stresa front" against German *anschluss* with Austria, which had raised its head the year before. Laval claimed to have won over the Prince of Wales to the idea of a deal with Mussolini.[2] Italian aggression

[1]Torrès, *op. cit.*, p. 135, to whom he said this personally.

[2]For his version of this curious incident see *Le Procès du Maréchal Pétain; compte rendu in extenso des audiences transmis par le Secrétariat Général de la Haute Cour de Justice* (1945), p. 184—henceforth referred to as *Le Procès Pétain.*

against Abyssinia continued, and after the League of Nations had condemned Mussolini for it and formally called for sanctions, there suddenly became known in December the famous "Hoare-Laval Pact". It planned to give Italy great concessions of territory in Abyssinia under the mask of a common control by France and England. Popular outcry in England forced the resignation of Sir Samuel Hoare and the scheme came to nothing. Mr. Ward Price records that "a month later Mussolini told me that he had been ready to accept them (i.e., the terms of the Hoare-Laval agreement) but had no time to say so before they were withdrawn".[1] Whatever the sincerity or utility of this subsequent profession, in the event the Abyssinian War went on, and evoked half-hearted "sanctions" from France and Britain. It was the cynical Lavalesque "realism" of the scheme which shocked British opinion, though it aroused very much less reaction in France.[2]

The pattern of European relationships which Laval had evolved in his own mind is, in part at least, indicated in his defence of 1945. He says that he had urged Mussolini not to go to war. He describes the secret "military alliance" which he had made with Italy "to defend Italy and France against a German invasion of Austria", and which he regarded as forming "a bridge leading to all those countries of Western and Eastern Europe which were then our allies". But the invocation of sanctions brought with it a wave of anti-fascist feeling in France which was "most unfortunate, for the anti-fascist feeling was to become stronger than the desire to preserve peace".[3]

[1]G. Ward Price, *op. cit.*, p. 238.
[2]Cf. Alexander Werth, *op. cit.*, p. 201.
[3]*The Unpublished Diary*, p. 34.

His fundamental desire was to keep international relations within the realm of diplomatic manoeuvre and subtle negotiation, and to prevent their breaking down into open hostilities: a desire which was, of course, shared by many other national leaders in France and in other countries. To anchor them within the shallows of diplomacy and stop their being tossed into the deep waters of war, he began to visualize a "Latin bloc", hinging on France and Italy but comprising also Spain, and linking up in turn with Britain and the United States in the west, and with Russia and the Balkan countries in the east. He believed, as he said in the Chamber, that "peace is fragile": he also believed, and said, that "there can be no solid peace in Europe without a Franco-German *rapprochement*".

There is little doubt that his very long delay in securing parliamentary ratification of the Franco-Soviet Pact (it was not in fact fully ratified until after he was out of power) did much to frustrate its purpose. It gave Germany time to launch a massive campaign against it, and to tear up Locarno by occupying and remilitarizing the Rhineland between its ratification by the Chamber and its ratification by the Senate. Russia was given little encouragement to place any trust in a Pact which met with so lukewarm and dilatory a reception in France; though it is always arguable that she would have placed little trust in it anyhow, and that even Laval could not have delayed Hitler's carefully timed programme of aggressions.[1]

But Laval's personal allergy to clear-cut political principles and his affection for the half-lights of twilight diplomacy probably produced the worst of

[1]Cf. Alexander Werth, *op. cit.*, p. 208.

both worlds, as constant effort to get the best of both worlds so frequently does. He incurred the risks of the Soviet Treaty but drew none of its potential advantages; he supported England in applying "sanctions", but forfeited Italian amenability without inspiring any Italian respect; he raised the ghost of a "Latin bloc" but never achieved the substance of it; he preserved the formalities of concerted action with Britain but succeeded only in arousing her profound distrust of his schemes. This, in sum, is the final condemnation of any foreign policy: that it failed so completely to achieve any of its avowed or implicit purposes.

So far as Laval evolved any philosophy of the international situation, it seems to have been roughly this. After 1870 it became increasingly impossible for France to achieve security by the sheer preponderance of her own resources and power. Her security depended basically upon her relations with her two big neighbours, Great Britain and Germany. France has remained the greatest land-power in western Europe, next to Germany, and the greatest naval power in western Europe, next to Britain. Her relations with other countries such as Italy, Russia, the United States, are determined ultimately by her relations with her two nearest and greatest neighbours. Given hostility between Britain and Germany, France must choose between them: and if she does not want to choose, she must try to prevent hostility between them. But given conditions of hostility between them, as after 1933, there were only two realistic courses open to France: either to treat Germany as her inevitable enemy, and so throw in her lot utterly with Britain, paying, if need be, the highest price for an Anglo-

French Alliance; or else to regard British help in time of need as too uncertain or too belated to be adequate for French security, and so to come to terms with Germany, if need be paying the highest price required for a Franco-German Alliance. Because British policy in the 1930's was ambiguous, wavering between sanctions and appeasement, between the policy of the Anglo-German Naval Agreement of 1935 and the policy of resistance to fascist aggression, the arguments of those who urged full *rapprochement* with Germany must hold the field. And this is what he tried to do. There is little doubt that even Laval, like so many other French leaders, would have preferred agreement with Britain; and still more would have preferred not to have to choose between these two alternative courses. But Laval's sense of realism told him that the choice must in the end be made, though it is difficult to ascertain how early he reached this conclusion. It was probably only after he left office at the beginning of 1936, when the dropping of the Hoare-Laval Pact, the Anglo-German Naval Agreement, and the growing might of Nazi Germany forced him to the conclusion almost in spite of himself: for he was never a man to abandon alternatives until he was compelled to. Nor is it suggested that at that time he would have formulated his analysis of the situation as clearly as this, nor was it one which he devised for himself. It was simply that by temperament, by general ignorance of foreign affairs, and by bitter experience, he became more and more susceptible to this argument, put forward most strongly and persistently by men like de Brinon and the Franco-German Committee. It prepared him for the same argument in 1940, after

Dunkirk: though it did not lead him to approve of the Munich Pact of 1938, which in fact was the logical historical consequence of the beliefs he seems to have held in the years between 1936 and 1940.

The political outlook of Laval between 1936 and 1940 is peculiarly difficult to follow. Though a member of the Senate, and of its Foreign Affairs Committee, he played no decisive role in the dramatic and disastrous events of these years. M. Torrès, whose biography—though hostile—is otherwise so illuminating on Laval's career, tails off significantly when he deals with this phase. The story is more than usually littered with mere gossip, save for occasional parliamentary speeches of Laval's which are almost the only reliable documentary material. Even the official "Act of Accusation" against him slid over these years with remarkable vagueness in the phrase: "Overthrown in January, 1936, after the failure of his plan to settle the Ethiopian crisis, he was animated by a hatred of England, which he held responsible for his downfall, and with a hatred of the French Parliament whose confidence he was unable to regain." Laval's retort was that though regretting the failure of the Hoare-Laval Pact, he had no special reason to hate England:[1] but he made it clear that he henceforth clung more stubbornly than ever to the thesis that peace would come only from a Franco-German *rapprochement*. The minor role which he played in these years when he held no ministerial post calls for no special examination: there is plenty to examine in his behaviour after the making of the armistice with Germany in June, 1940.

* * * * *

[1] *The Unpublished Diary*, pp. 31f.

When war broke out in September, 1939, Laval lay low. But he was by no means inactive. With his acute sense of impending crisis, he was manoeuvring for his own return to power. His efforts since 1936 had all failed, but he sensed that a more suitable moment might be approaching. In October, 1939, the political intrigues against M. Daladier's ministry were numerous. On 26th October, M. Élie-J. Bois published in the *Petit Parisien* an article aimed at bringing into the open the leading intriguers against Daladier and against the continuation of the war after the rapid collapse of Poland. Ribbentrop had made a speech at Dantzig which was designed to woo France whilst attacking England. "Well then," asked Bois, "what information can his spies be sending him? Because there are four schemers who champ their bits in the byways which lead to power, and who criticize and make lists with their names in prominent positions, who compromise honourable and glorious names. . . ." This evoked a telephone-call from Laval and an invitation to have a talk in his little office in the Champs-Élysées. "I ask that the war shall be carried on until victory," said Laval, "but I contend that the goal cannot be reached with the present Government. . . . No one can do it but a man who stands out above the scrum. I am not, as you might say, very thick with Pétain, but I saw Goering saluting him at Cracow at Pilsudski's funeral. I know his prestige. His name would suffice to rally round him the best and most energetic men. There'd be some glamour about it. That's what upset me about your article. . . . You understand, it would be a great pity if he were discredited in advance by being made to appear in the light of a future Premier in a 'peace at any price' Cabinet." When Bois protested that Pétain showed every sign of being old and feeble, Laval retorted, "That doesn't matter. What will be asked of him? To be a statue on a pedestal. His name! His prestige! Nothing more."[1] Bois concluded, correctly, that Laval was already busy manoeuvring in every direction to become "the man of the situation".

But what other inferences can be convincingly drawn from this important evidence of Laval's plans? The idea of Pétain as a right-wing leader in politics was not new. In 1935 a pamphlet was widely circulated bearing the title *We Want Pétain*; its author was Gustave Hervé, one of Laval's early pre-1914 acquaintances, and it expressed the views of the *Action française* group of Charles Maurras.[2] It outlined a plan of an authoritarian regime, and hinted that the right moment for a *coup d'état* would be "in wartime, and especially in a moment of defeat". It was, indeed, a remarkably prophetic pamphlet, and the strongest plank in the otherwise very thin evidence that Vichy rested on a long-premeditated conspiracy. There is no evidence that Laval had in any way prompted this pamphlet, nor even that he had read it:[3] but it seems clear enough that the ideas it contained, much canvassed again in the autumn of 1939, struck him as the basis of a timely manoeuvre on his own part to find "a statue on a pedestal" which should preside over his own return to power in the moment of France's greatest need. He must have known that,

[1] Élie-J. Bois, *op. cit.*, pp. 136f.

[2] *C'est Pétain qu'il nous faut* (1935).

[3] In the course of his evidence at the trial of Marshal Pétain, Laval admitted that in 1935 he favoured these ideas. See *Le Procès Pétain*, pp. 184–5.

whether it failed or succeeded, it would be the most dangerous and most spectacular *coup* of his whole life.

On the evidence of this interview, and on very much more flimsy evidence contained in Anatole de Monzie's highly suspect book *Ci-Devant*, which appeared in Paris in June, 1941, there has been elaborated the thesis that the whole complex process which includes the appointment of Pétain as Vice-President of the Council of Ministers in Paul Reynaud's cabinet on 19th May, Reynaud's resignation and the negotiations of the armistice with Germany in June, the overthrow of the Third Republic and the conferment of power on Pétain in July, was in fact one vast conspiracy, engineered by Pierre Laval with the connivance of Pétain's personal friends and other defeatists. Indeed, some would even include the military defeat and collapse of France in May within this conspiracy. This is not the place to analyse all the frailties and fallacies of this theory, which seemed plausible enough to many distressed Frenchmen in the agony of 1940. It is important to remember, however, that to show that these events all worked to the advantage of Pétain and Laval and were broadly in conformity with ideas which they had long held is not in itself to prove that they deliberately engineered this sequence of events. It was natural enough, in conditions of defeat and supreme crisis, that the men whose outlook had been for a long time defeatist and whose policy was known to favour *rapprochement* with Germany should appear to have been proved right and should be accorded power. The theory of the conspiracy attributes to Laval, above all, a superhuman degree of foresight and of diabolical control over events—and that at a time when events had got peculiarly out of control—which his previous career scarcely bears out.[1] The many deep forces of despair and defeatism which existed in certain high levels of French life were spontaneously mobilized and brought to the front: that Laval, and to some extent Pétain, tried to ride these forces, and that they came into power at Vichy on the crest of these forces, is true enough. Given their outlook, it would have been foolish of them had they not done so. But there is no evidence that in order to achieve power they had deliberately worked for France's defeat, even though there is considerable evidence that once defeat had happened, Pétain worked to usc it for a separate peace, and Laval for the establishment of a new form of emergency government of which he was himself the controller.

The chronological sequence of events is important if Laval's precise significance in it is to be understood. The Germans broke through on the Meuse by 15th May, 1940. On 19th May Pétain was made Vice-President of the Council and Minister of State in Reynaud's government. By 10th June the German armies were sweeping down on Paris and the government evacuated to Tours. In the cabinet meeting at Tours, on 12th–13th June, Pétain and Weygand urged a separate armistice with Germany, but were outvoted. The government moved on to Bordeaux, and

[1]Cf. especially the anonymous pamphlet, *Pétain-Laval, The Conspiracy*, translated by Michael Sadleir, September, 1942, most of which had appeared serially in *France*, the French daily paper then published in London. It was of course a thesis much favoured by the Free French and by all the most fervent anti-Vichy forces (cf. Vincent Auriol: *Hier Demain* (1945), I, pp. 59–154); and by the American journalist, the late Mr. H. R. Knickerbocker: *Is To-morrow Hitler's?* (1941). For further discussion of it see my *Democracy in France* (1946), Chapter VI.

it was there on 16th June that there took place the decisive cabinet meeting, when Reynaud resigned and advised President Lebrun to ask Marshal Pétain to form a new government. Laval did not come on to the scene of actual operations until he arrived at Bordeaux on 15th June. Until then he had been living at home in Chateldon. Pétain proposed to make Laval Minister of Foreign Affairs, but because of the intervention of General Weygand and M. Charles-Roux, Secretary-General at the Quai d'Orsay, Laval was at first excluded.[1] In the course of the night of 16th–17th, Pétain asked Hitler for an armistice and on 17th broadcast the announcement that he had asked Hitler for it "in honour, as between soldiers". It was duly signed on 22nd June. It was not until 23rd June that President Lebrun agreed to appoint Laval Minister of State without portfolio. Again, as between 1936 and 1939, Laval's alibi is complete: he held no post of ministerial responsibility whilst the crucial negotiation of the armistice was taking place.

The reasons for his belated inclusion in the ministry are interesting. According to Paul Baudouin, Marshal Pétain said, "I could not do anything else. . . . I must have him in the Government for his intrigues will be less dangerous here than if he was raising opposition

[1]See F. Charles-Roux, *Cinq Mois Tragiques aux Affaires Étrangères* (1949), pp. 48ff; J. Weygand, *The Role of General Weygand* (1948), p. 143; Albert Lebrun, *Témoignage* (1946), p. 86; *Le Procès Laval*, p. 212; and Paul Baudouin, *The Private Diaries* (1948), pp. 118ff., where the story is told in detail. Laval later had something to thank them for, because his exclusion enabled him to make much, in his defence in 1945, of the fact that he had not been a member of the government which asked for the armistice, which was of course completely true. He made it no secret, either in 1940 or in 1945, that he supported capitulation, but could argue that he would have made better terms than those which Pétain and Baudouin actually accepted. It may well be that he would have bargained harder and got more.

outside."[1] He had, in fact, spent a feverish fortnight in generating pressure to insert himself into the ministry, and in the end Pétain had considerable difficulty in getting even Lebrun to agree to his inclusion. He thus came into the ministry as something of an intruder, against the wishes and inclinations of Lebrun, Weygand, Baudouin, and to some extent Pétain himself—scarcely the position of the central figure on a vast deliberate conspiracy which extended back some two months.

The spirit which Laval immediately imported into the cabinet was one of bitter hostility towards Britain. The recent broadcasts of General de Gaulle and of Mr. Churchill, together with the departure of the British Ambassador from France,[2] seem to have convinced him that French policy, now committed to finding a *modus vivendi* with a victorious Germany, should follow a harsh line of hostility towards Britain. "A violent scene between Laval and myself then followed", writes Baudouin, "for he advocated a break with England while I opposed it. I told the Marshal that if he adopted Laval's point of view I would resign, and, what was much more serious, General Weygand and Admiral Darlan would resign with me. The Marshal told Laval to calm himself. . . ."[3] "M. Pierre Laval

[1] *The Private Diaries of Paul Baudouin*, pp. 138–40. There is some slight discrepancy between the exact details given by Baudouin and those given by Charles-Roux (*op. cit.*, p. 95), but the essentials are identical. Laval's own comment was, "At long last, and after much discussion, I was asked to share with M. Camille Chautemps the post of Vice-President of the Council of Ministers" (*The Unpublished Diary*, p. 40).

[2] The British Ambassador, Sir Ronald Campbell, was not formally "withdrawn". In July, 1940, Lord Halifax sent a telegram to the French Government in which he explained this, adding that Sir Ronald's only instructions had been to avoid falling into the hands of the enemy. Cf. Baudouin, *op. cit.*, p. 137; Charles-Roux, *op. cit.*, p. 91.

[3] Baudouin, *op. cit.*, p. 139.

gave vent to a violent anti-English outburst, and asked for the immediate recall of our ambassador. I advised moderation, and I said that during the past twenty years French policy had suffered only too much from allowing itself to be carried away by ideologies and prejudices."[1] M. Charles-Roux confirms this clash of views, adding "the entry of M. Laval into governmental circles occurred all the more inopportunely in that the causes of friction with England went on multiplying."[2] British attacks on the French fleet at Oran and Mers-el-Kébir, and Gaullist attempts on Dakar, soon followed. Large areas of French Equatorial Africa (Chad and the Cameroons) were won over to the Free French. These events, in fast and dramatic sequence, brought Britain and Vichy to the brink of open hostilities: and this at a time, it must be remembered, when most people in France, as in Europe generally, believed that the war was nearly over, that Britain would soon be forced to follow France's lead and make peace with Germany and Italy, and that the era of Hitler's "New Order" in Europe was about to begin. It is certain that Laval believed all this, for not only did he base his actions on it but he later admitted that he had believed it. "Do you believe that in 1940", he asked at the trial of Pétain, "anyone with common sense could imagine anything but the victory of Germany?"[3] The most important immediate consequence of this belief—shared by many well-informed people overseas as well as in Europe, and expressed by the French military leaders in the famous prediction that Britain would

[1] *Ibid.*, p. 139.
[2] Roux, *op. cit.*, p. 96.
[3] *Le Procès Pétain*, p. 195; *Le Procès Laval*, p. 88.

have "her neck wrung like a chicken in six weeks"—was that it was assumed that the armistice, and the provisional dictatorial Pétainist regime created by it, would be very short-lived. Peace-terms between France and Germany would have to be made in a matter of a few months: and the immediate task was to manoeuvre into the most favourable position for making terms. It was a situation in which Laval was convinced that he, more than any other French leader, could make the best bargain. We miss entirely the whole purport of his policy during the last six months of 1940 if we overlook the conviction prevailing at Vichy that this, and no other, was their supreme task in 1940. There was, therefore, even a certain merit and perhaps a real diplomatic advantage in being on very bad terms with Britain. Those, like Charles-Roux, who felt ties of loyalty to France's ally, and others, like the silky Paul Baudouin, who were already *attentiste* enough to want to move more cautiously, resisted the drift towards active hostilities between France and Britain. Others, led by Laval and embittered by British attacks on the fleet, saw in the drift an opportunity to win favour for themselves and for France in the forthcoming Nazi "New Order". "Like everyone else", Laval wrote in 1945, "I believed that the German occupation would last only a relatively short while."[1]

There arises, for these early weeks of the Vichy government, the question of what responsibility Laval bore for the decision not to continue the war from North Africa, and for the procedure by which the rump of the National Assembly conferred absolute

[1] *The Unpublished Diary*, p. 67; and cf. pp. 45, 63.

powers on Marshal Pétain. Chapter V of the "Act of Accusation" charged him with major responsibility for both decisions. It is an important question for any judgment of Laval and of his significance: was he, in short, as nearly all his most hostile critics have maintained, the architect of the Vichy government? Was it indeed he, more than any other single man, who blocked all further official resistance to Germany after the armistice, and who devised the peculiar structure of Vichy which kept Pétain "on the pedestal"?

Laval was on safe ground when he insisted that the armistice had been decided upon before he entered the government, and even when he blamed the makers of it for not having "protested solemnly against those clauses of the Armistice Convention which rendered it inapplicable", so that subsequent discussions and negotiations about the precise interpretation of it might be begun. He declared—and no doubt sincerely, for it is precisely what he would have done—that "Had I been in the Government at that time I would have insisted upon having, if nothing better could have been obtained, at least a protocol outlining the conditions in which the armistice was to be applied."[1] He admitted that he had no faith in the utility of the President or Ministers going to North Africa, but contended that it was lack of will on the part of the government, and lack of effective transport arrangements, which prevented their going, not his own arguments. He has been accused of having lobbied the members of the Assembly at Bordeaux, of having intimidated President Lebrun, and of having

[1] *The Unpublished Diary*, p. 42.

frustrated the attempt of some of the deputies, on the *Massilia*, actually to transplant the government to Africa.[1]

There seems to be no doubt that he did play a leading part in these events. To establish a provisional French government to attend to French interests, based on the terms of the newly concluded armistice, and to prevent continuation of the war from a base overseas, was certainly his main purpose at this time. It was this desire which formed the common ground with Marshal Pétain, and which made their collaboration at Vichy possible. He would naturally and inevitably, in the confused conditions of June and July, 1940, be active in lobbying parliamentarians and in forming delegations of like-minded politicians. But his own criticism of what has been credited to him has substance in it. "It is difficult to imagine", he writes, "how I could have exercised such power as a mere member of Parliament. The truth is that amongst those who might have left for North Africa there was a complete lack of will or wish to depart. Had it been otherwise it must seem that I had almost supernatural powers of persuasion. . . . I should never have allowed myself to be dissuaded by the opposition of a few members of Parliament, particularly when this opposition was merely verbal. . . . Had the opposition

[1]E.g., Élie-J. Bois, *op. cit.*, p. 413; Torrès, *op. cit.*, p. 173; Tissier, *op. cit.*, p. 43; all deriving mainly from the book of Jean Montigny, *Toute La Vérité*, which it was alleged was written at Laval's own instigation! Jean Thouvenin, *La France Nouvelle* (1941) tells a similar story of Laval's successful intrigues. A. Kammerer, *La Vérité sur l'Armistice* (1944), p. 207, follows completely the account by Montigny, according to which a delegation of a dozen parliamentarians, representing a hundred of their colleagues and led by Laval, waited upon President Lebrun and dissuaded him from his intention of sailing to Africa. According to Lebrun (*op. cit.*, pp. 91f.) it was a wildly excited and gesticulating party, and has often been falsely described; see also Lebrun's evidence in *Le Procès Laval*, pp. 209–17.

continued, I should have ignored it."[1] He is surely right in insisting that, as he held no ministerial office at this time (before 23rd June, 1940), the responsibility for not having continued the war from North Africa must rest on President Lebrun and the Cabinet; and if they allowed themselves to be talked out of it by Laval or by anyone else, that in no way absolves them from responsibility.

Nor can Laval be blamed for propagating his own views at a time when all men were thrown into complete confusion and disorganization, when communications were broken and the world that was France seemed to be crashing to the ground. As usual, he knew precisely what *he* wanted, and was strenuously energetic in trying to get it: it would have been better for France had more men equally had the strength of their convictions, and the energy to pursue a clear policy. In these conditions it is hypocritical to censure Laval for pursuing what he believed to be best with boundless vigour—it was what Hitler, Churchill and General de Gaulle were all doing too. It is only *what* he was seeking which can be censured, not his energy in seeking it. He never ceased to proclaim the belief, from 1940 until his death, that it was not in the greater interests of France to "abandon it to the cruel domination of the conqueror rather than to make the attempt which, in fact, was made to hold off the conqueror by negotiation, thus attempting to lighten, to some extent at least, the load of suffering and hardship". The strongest case for Pétain's policy, made at the time, and throughout the four years of Vichy rule, and at his trial in 1945, was that it

[1] *The Unpublished Diary*, p. 42; *Le Procès Petain*, p. 187; *Le Procès Laval* p. 71.

was better to have a French government, however precarious and partial its independence, surviving on French soil, than to abandon metropolitan soil entirely to direct German administration. This difference was always tacitly admitted, even in the gibe "Veni, vidi, Vichy". Nor, as we shall see, was Vichy by any means the passive and docile tool of German policy. It had from the first, and in the course of time, until the end of 1942, it augmented, certain elements of real independence. One may not like what it did or was hoping to do in the way of social reorganization and authoritarian government: but at least it was not the obedient agent of German government, as Hitler subsequently found to his chagrin and cost.[1]

The incident of the *Massilia* remains wrapped in a certain obscurity. Charles Pomaret, Pétain's Minister of the Interior and a supporter of the armistice who was later imprisoned by Laval, gives the most illuminating account of it. He accuses Admiral Darlan of hatching a deliberate plot to discredit the parliamentarians by presenting them as deserters and cowards. The *Massilia* had on board Daladier, Mandel, Viénot, Campinchi, Mendès-France, Delbos and a dozen other parliamentarians. It sailed from Bordeaux on 19th June and reached Casablanca on 24th June—two days after the signing of the armistice. Finding their attempt to carry on resistance overseas frustrated, they tried to return. But they did not succeed in arriving back in France until too late to

[1]The note of "standing by a crippled France" was struck, with considerable effect, in a *communiqué* issued on the day of the armistice: it exactly expresses Pétain's position. "The Government has considered it its duty to stay in France, to share the fate of all Frenchmen, and (believes) that France can only rise again through composure, order and work." It may well have been Laval who expressed this more pithily—"You can't defend France by leaving her." Cf. *Le Procès Pétain*, p. 187.

take part in the vote of July 10th, which conferred plenary powers on Marshal Pétain. They had, it appeared, been got safely out of the way during the crucial parliamentary session—the last of the Third Republic: and they had, incidentally, been made to appear slightly ridiculous. Lebrun, Herriot and Jeanneney, the President of the Republic and the two Presidents of the Chambers, were retained in France despite their original notion of departing. It indeed looked like a deep-laid plot.

But again it must be recalled that Laval held no ministerial post at the time when the *Massilia* sailed from Bordeaux, and if there were any governmental plot to ship inconvenient members of the National Assembly out of the way it could have been hatched and executed only by Marshal Pétain, Admiral Darlan or Paul Baudouin, or at least with their full knowledge and connivance: and again it is they who must bear responsibility for any such conspiracy. But the evidence that there was in fact a deliberate plot is extremely scanty and ambiguous. M. Bois wrote of the "*Massilia* trap" and hinted at Paul Baudouin's responsibility for it: but he gave no concrete evidence. Laval is reported to have boasted that he prevented the Government's departure to Perpignan, which was what Paul Baudouin, on June 19th, is said to have assured Lord Lloyd and Mr. Alexander it would do, *en route* for Africa: but there is no evidence either that Laval did so boast, or that Baudouin acted in bad faith in what he said.[1] As Charles-Roux suggests, sheer confusion was the simplest explanation.[2] On the other hand, the fate of the parliamentarians in Morocco

[1]Cf. Baudouin, *op. cit.*, pp. 127–30.
[2]Charles-Roux, *op. cit.*, pp. 77–8.

seems to have been partially sealed by Laval. "News had been received from Morocco", wrote Baudouin on 27th June, "that M. Mandel had compromised himself with the British representatives and the British Minister of Information; in view of this, and of General de Gaulle's appeals by wireless from London, Laval had decided that an examination must be made as into a plot against the safety of the State."[1] Mandel, most active of the opponents of the armistice and of Pétain's government, had been arrested on 17th June, for one morning, at Bordeaux, only to be released again with apologies from the Marshal. On his arrival in Morocco on 24th he and other "bellicists" were arrested again, and this may well have been at the orders of Laval, as they suspected at the time.[2] The role of Laval grew steadily in importance from this time onwards: and events which had hitherto played into his hands can now be more convincingly attributed to his machinations. His silence on the fate of the *Massilia* in his *Diary* is a suggestive one.

However disputable Laval's domination of events before 23rd June, it is indisputable that he took an extremely active and leading role in the political revolution of July 10th–11th which overthrew the Third Republic and constituted the curious stop-gap regime of Marshal Pétain. His relative lack of direct responsibility for the course of events before 23rd June only enhances his sense of opportunism and his shrewdness of judgment from that time onwards. He grasped all the essentials of the immediate situation

[1]Baudouin, *op. cit.*, p. 150.

[2]Maurice Martin du Gard, *La Carte Impériale* (1949), Chapter I, gives a vivid account of the affair; and cf. A. Kammerer, *La Vérité sur l'Armistice* pp. 198–203.

and exploited them with the utmost vigour and enterprise for his own ends: it was the long-range and more moral forces—such as Britain's capacity to resist Germany—which characteristically evaded him, and which in the end upset all his "realistic" calculations. But as a political opportunist his judgment of the immediate situation was shrewd and penetrating.

Baudouin's description of Laval's attitude, even when some allowance is made for self-exculpation on the part of the writer, is broadly true. "On our way out from the Marshal", he writes on 26th June, "we . . . were buttonholed by Pierre Laval, who had been waiting for us. He explained the reasons why it seemed necessary to him to give the Marshal exceptional constitutional powers. It was impossible to govern with Parliament, especially with the Front Populaire Chamber of 1936. 'This Chamber has made me sick,' he said: 'Now it is I who am going to make it sick.' Bouthillier and I agreed that in the circumstances exceptional powers were called for, and it was only possible to govern by decree during a long prorogation of Parliament. 'That is not enough,' replied Pierre Laval. 'We must revise the Constitution, and put an end to the present political system.' "[1] Despite the opposition of Baudouin and General Weygand and the hesitations of Pétain and Lebrun, Laval successfully pressed his own scheme for a positive reform of the Constitution. "I will make a strong effort", he told Pétain, "to obtain the full consent of Albert Lebrun to his disappearance."[2] An hour later he

[1]Baudouin, *op. cit.*, pp. 148–154.

[2]President Lebrun later insisted (*op. cit.*, p. 112) that his own effacement was the result of the passing of the Law, and so was the act of the National Assembly and not of Pétain or Laval.

reported his complete success with Lebrun; and Pétain agreed to let him try his hand. It meant summoning and lobbying the National Assembly so as to produce the necessary majority of 467 senators and deputies for a revision of the constitution of the Republic. "The Marshal", records Baudouin, "looked at him with admiration and astonishment." Laval, indeed, now held the reins.

Laval's relations with Marshal Pétain were never easy, and were subject to recurrent storms and explosions on either side. He was consistently opposed and bitterly hated by men like General Weygand and Admiral Darlan, with whom, as professional servicemen, the Marshal was more naturally sympathetic. It was suggested in the course of the Pétain trial that one of Laval's most effective contacts with Pétain was through his son-in-law, Count René de Chambrun. Chambrun, as a direct descendant of Lafayette, enjoyed the unusual privilege of being both a citizen of France and a citizen of the United States. Before the war he had been secretary of the *Comité France-Amérique*, of which Marshal Pétain was president. Their personal relations had remained both good and constant, and it would be surprising had Laval failed to utilize this obvious and very useful channel of influence with the Marshal.[1] On the other hand, it would be incorrect to think only in terms of the austere, simple-minded octogenarian Marshal being subjected to the wiles of the scheming politician. The Marshal had a slyness of his own at times, and he sometimes took severe precautions to withstand Laval's intrigues: as witness the letter which he made Laval sign, in

[1] *Le Procès Pétain*, p. 375.

November, 1942, reserving certain powers to the Marshal himself, even while augmenting the powers of Laval.[1] The shiftiness and unreliability of the Marshal's decisions were a constant source of anxiety to all his ministers. But in July, 1940, Laval's chief concern was to secure unlimited powers for Pétain himself. The statue had to be erected on its pedestal.

Laval and Alibert (who a few days later became Minister of Justice) drafted the constitutional measures to be passed by the Assembly. On 9th July the Assembly met at Vichy to ratify the armistice. Nearly 650 members (out of its 932) were able to attend, and a majority voted for ratification. Next day Laval, in a secret session, promoted a resolution investing the government of Marshal Pétain with provisional plenary powers until a "new constitution" should be promulgated. 569 parliamentarians voted for it, and only 80 against it, with 17 formal abstentions.[2] The "new constitution of the French State" was to be "ratified by the nation and brought into application by the Assemblies which it creates". It had the merits of leaving both courses wide open: until the war were over, promulgation of the "new constitution" could be simply postponed, and meanwhile the old National Assembly and the Presidential powers of Albert Lebrun had ceased to exist; when the war was over (in the expected few weeks) Pétain's government would be left with a free hand to devise whatever constitution it preferred, subject to "ratification by the

[1] *Ibid.*, p. 262 and Annexe VIII.

[2] Vivid descriptions of how Laval out-manoeuvred the rival proposal of Taurines and his *Anciens combattants* group to suspend the existing Constitution are given by J. Paul-Boncour, *Entre Deux Guerres*, Vol. III, Chap. IV, and Vincent Auriol, *Hier-Demain*, Vol. I, pp. 93–139. And see Gordon Wright, *The Reshaping of French Democracy* (1950), pp. 23–26.

nation". It gave Laval all the power he wanted and needed immediately, and held out the prospect of a complete overhaul of the political system in the not very distant future. In fact, Vichy survived for four years by dint of never promulgating the new constitution: so even formally it was a stop-gap regime.[1]

Utilizing his new powers, Marshal Pétain's first "Constitutional Act" was to abrogate the famous "Wallon Amendment" of 1875 which had defined the powers of the President of the Republic, and to declare himself "Chief of the French State". This combination of supreme executive power with constitution-making power made Vichy a personal dictatorship, claiming a direct mandate from the National Assembly: a novel and ingenious basis for dictatorship, and the basis of the subsequent so-called "National Revolution". The cloak of legitimacy with which the Vichy regime thus invested itself was to be of supreme importance in retaining the loyalty and devotion of most of the chief colonial administrators overseas, who in the midst of so much political confusion were only too ready to escape from crucial political dilemmas by proclaiming their allegiance to the "only legitimate government" of metropolitan France.[2] It also enabled the men of Vichy to present General de Gaulle and the succession of resistance organizations hinging upon him as "dissidents" and usurpers. Despite the ingenious and clever legalistic

[1]Pétain did get drafted a "new Constitution" but insisted that it could be promulgated only from Paris after its liberation: Philippe Pétain, *Quatre Années au Pouvoir* (1949), pp. 147ff.

[2]The best example of this is to be seen in Admiral Decoux, who was Governor-General of Indo-China. See Decoux, *A la Barre de l'Indo-Chine (1940–1945)* (1949), esp. p. 360. See also Maurice Martin du Gard, *op. cit.*, Chapter VI, for the corresponding attitude of Pierre Boisson, Governor of French West Africa.

arguments of Professor René Cassin and others, it was always extremely difficult for the Gaullists to present themselves as more entitled to be the "legitimate" government of France than the men of Vichy.[1]

There remained one great anxiety. Pétain was already 84 years old. The succession—the problem of all dictatorships—must be arranged. Already by 6th July, Laval was busy with his plans, as Paul Baudouin records. "I lunched with Pierre Laval. He was very concerned with the problem of the Marshal's successor, and he wished to appear in the eyes of the National Assembly as designated by the Marshal to carry out the constitutional reform if he could not do it himself. . . . In the middle of the afternoon I told the Marshal of Pierre Laval's point of view, and he showed himself by no means enthusiastic over the idea of appointing his eventual successor."[2] Baudouin and others wished General Weygand to be nominated: but Laval had only to make "a firm request" to the Marshal, and it was Laval who was nominated "dauphin" as well as Vice-President of the Council of Ministers. He remained in that unenviable but—to him—crucial position until 13th December, 1940; and on October 28th, he also succeeded Baudouin as Minister of Foreign Affairs. Meantime, it was a reinsurance measure against the reversal of all his plans by the untimely death of the Marshal. The disappointed General Weygand remarked, "I should never have expected that the marriage of a Marshal of France with the Republic would produce such progeny as Pierre Laval."[3]

[1]The Gaullist case appeared in René Cassin, *Un coup d'état: la soi-disant constitution de Vichy* (1941).

[2]Baudouin, *op. cit.*, pp. 161f.; *Le Procès Pétain*, pp. 189–90.

[3]Charles-Roux, *op. cit.*, p. 164.

In all these developments Laval served as the real gravedigger of the Third Republic, and the chief architect of the Vichy regime. He even later admitted and rejoiced in these roles. "The decision of Parliament to confer on the Marshal all necessary powers for a sufficient period to permit the country's recovery was an honourable one. I merely shared this view with many others. If I was more active than some in seeking to implement this viewpoint it was because of my habit of working for the realisation of an object when I am convinced that it is a just one. . . . I was given the mission to discuss and defend the Government proposal before the two Houses separately and the National Assembly, and this I did by virtue of a specific mandate given me by the Marshal. . . . The fact that I succeeded—and anybody else would have succeeded had he been in my place—does not in any sense mean that I had to manoeuvre or intrigue. In order to justify this thesis it must be supposed that there was a majority in opposition to this proposal; in fact, the majority loudly demanded it, or it must be imagined that I had extraordinary powers of suggestion over the two Chambers. This, to say the least of it, would not have been very complimentary to those who should have crossed swords with me but who, in fact, remained stonily silent."[1] Here again, when allowance has been made for the incident of the *Massilia* which played into his hands, and for his own great skill in parliamentary lobbying and persuasion, it remains true that the 569 parliamentarians who voted power to Pétain must severally and collectively shoulder the ultimate responsibility, along with

[1]*The Unpublished Diary*, pp. 51, 55; *Le Procès Laval*, p. 71.

President Lebrun, for the installation of Pétain. Laval's peculiar offence was to know what he wanted more clearly than anyone else, and to pursue it with more vigour and verve than anyone else.

* * * * *

Between Laval's accession to power on 23rd June, and his temporary fall from power on 13th December, 1940, the whole position of France in relation to Germany, and perhaps the whole future of the world, were revolutionized by the Battle of Britain. The conspicuous failure of the Germans to establish such air superiority over the Channel as to secure either capitulation or invasion of the British Isles brought to an abrupt and dramatic end all the original assumptions on which Laval had worked in June and July: that the war was nearly over, that the armistice would before long give way to a peace-treaty, that France must adapt herself to the existence of the Nazi "New Order" in Europe. After October, 1940, it was obvious that the war would go on, that Britain was further than ever from capitulating, and that the Vichy government could begin to draw greater advantages than even Laval had at first expected from the embarrassments of Hitler. It is in this period that Laval seems to have conceived the idea of exploiting a certain balance in Europe between Germany and Britain in the west, and between Germany and Russia in the east. Supposing France were to supplant Italy as the second partner in the Axis? Germany and Russia were still nominally allies, under the Nazi-Soviet Pact of 1939; but it was evident that there were certain inevitable difficulties between them. The

German deadlock in the west gave Russia new opportunities. A stalemate peace between Germany and Britain could also, perhaps, be usefully exploited if France could serve as go-between. By October Hitler may have foreseen that this opportunity would tempt Laval, for he warned Laval at Montoire that "if England should offer a compromise peace I will not add to Germany's sufferings by sparing France." The old conceptions of international affairs which had guided Laval's policy in the years before the war began to raise their heads again. He admits the resurgence of these ideas at this time. "We were then defeated and in 1940 I did not believe that the defeat of Germany was probable. My duty was to reduce as much as possible the financial burden of our country which was the consequence of our defeat. . . . Without us Germany could not possibly organize Europe and it was clear to me that she would have to pay, in terms of our independence and our territorial integrity, a price for our co-operation. . . . Had the war ended at this time or at any time while Germany was allied to the Soviet Union, we would have had less to fear from German ambition. We would have been in a position to strike a balance of power by playing the Russian hand if Germany had attempted to establish hegemony in Europe."[1]

These conceptions showed themselves in the famous interviews at Montoire on 22nd and 24th October, 1940—immediately after the defeat of the *Luftwaffe* in the Battle of Britain. He claims that his aim was to prise loose Germany's stranglehold on France which she had secured by the terms of the armistice. Through

[1] *The Unpublished Diary*, p. 93.

Abetz, the German Ambassador in Paris, he arranged a meeting with Ribbentrop. On the way to this meeting he was told that he would also meet Hitler. Two days later he met them again, in company with Pétain. Marshal Pétain's report to his Ministers on his return seems to have been little more precise or communicative than the dull official statement which he published to the country. Hitler appears to have talked most of the time, economic collaboration was more than once vaguely broached, but nothing concrete was settled. "Everything remained obscure", remarked Baudouin, "and we were in a fog." "What seems certain is that some form of collaboration was promised, but of what nature we are ignorant." Laval insisted that he held his own with Hitler, and that the degree of economic collaboration hinted at was no more than was already required by Article 3 of the Armistice Convention. On 30th October, Pétain, in a broadcast, spoke of having "entered on to the path of collaboration". But the main gain from the meeting was concealed at the time, and it was Laval's. He had got Hitler to speak to him on equal terms: he had opened up some possibility of negotiations: and he had caused anxieties in Italy. On the day of the second Montoire meeting Count Ciano noted in his *Diary*, "During the evening von Ribbentrop telephones from a little railway station in France. He reports on conversations with Franco and with Pétain, and is, on the whole, satisfied with the results achieved. He says that the programme of collaboration is heading towards concrete results. I do not conceal my doubt and suspicion. Nevertheless, it is essential that the inclusion of France in the Axis shall not be to our detriment."[1] And a judgment on Montoire worthy of note is that of Renthe-Finck, Hitler's special diplomatic delegate to Vichy: "For me, Montoire constitutes the greatest defeat of the whole German policy towards France. We gained nothing from it, and nearly lost everything we had. We did not succeed in winning France over to our cause, nor in occupying the whole of French territory. If there had not been Montoire, there would probably not have been, either, an allied landing in North Africa, or our own *débâcle* there."[2] It is clear enough that Laval gave away nothing that mattered at Montoire: though no doubt he used sly and at times honeyed words.

This policy of ostensible collaboration but of manœuvre for a compromise or stalemate peace marked, increasingly, his attitude after the Battle of Britain. Baudouin shared his essential views, even whilst quarrelling with him to the point of handing in his own resignation. But he believed, as did Laval, that "what we can do is to work out a *modus vivendi* in the economic field for the period of the armistice; also, if the Germans so desire, to try, with the feeble means at our disposal, to bridge the gulf between the German and Anglo-Saxon worlds in order to arrive at peace".[3] Laval's means to this end were characteristically direct and *outrancier*. He expressed to Germans great impatience for the defeat of

[1]*Ciano's Diary*, p. 300. Cf. *Ciano's Diplomatic Papers* (1948), pp. 400–1. According to Ciano, Laval claimed that for the moment he must confine himself to defending himself in Africa, and used "the usual arguments of raw materials and the needs of French commerce".

[2]Quoted from an interview given to *La Libre Belgique*, 1 and 2 November, 1947, in Pétain, *Quatre Années au Pouvoir*, p. 70*n*. See also Charles-Roux, *op. cit.*, pp. 369–83; *Le Procès Pétain*, pp. 194–6 and 208; *Le Procès Laval*, pp. 222–24; text in W. L. Langer, *Our Vichy Gamble* (1947), pp. 94-6.

[3]Baudouin, *op. cit.*, p. 264.

England: though he sometimes accompanied it with a sly sting. "When you get to London with your army", he remarked to a German journalist, "send me a postcard."[1] He always counted flattery and vague expressions of friendliness as the loose change of diplomacy: costing him nothing, yet perhaps winning him concrete advantages in return. In June, 1942, he said publicly, "I foresee a German victory." In the trial of Pétain in 1945 he explained that he had originally written, "I believe in a German victory and foresee it", but amended it at the direction of Pétain.[2] In his *Diary* he was at pains to explain the advantages this statement won for him in negotiations with Sauckel and other Germans, and how it helped to cut the ground from under the collaborationists of Paris who were so busy attacking him at that time. This rings true. He was quite prepared to say as many nice things to the Germans, and even about the Germans in public, as would be likely to make them believe in his good faith, and as would encourage them to go on negotiating with him. Never did Machiavelli have a more faithful disciple than Pierre Laval. What cannot be won by force may be won by fraud: does not every nation's secret service work on the same principle?

Characteristically, too, he never took seriously those measures for achieving a "National Revolution" on which Pétain, Weygand, Baudouin and others were so keen. Their semi-mystical talk of national regeneration through suffering, of France

[1]Charles-Roux, *op. cit.*, p. 207, where the point of the barb is completely missed. "Even the German", he reports, "appeared shocked."

[2]*Le Procès Pétain*, pp. 200–205. The careful consideration given to Laval's famous statement shows how it was deliberately made by Laval as a "plant", for future quotation to the Germans when they should doubt his intentions in negotiations with them; and he duly made this use of it in dealing with Abetz and Sauckel.

doing penance for past sins through a disciplined ascetic regeneration, repelled him. He regarded it with an amused tolerance, as being possibly helpful in blending France more harmoniously into the landscape of a Nazi "New Order", but as not to be treated seriously in operation. His hard-headed political "realism", his concentration on the mechanics of power and on manipulation of the levers of governmental control, his faith in his own diplomatic artistry in negotiation, all precluded any concern for the more fanciful elements of the "Labour Charter" and the slogan of "Work, Family, Fatherland". He went out of his way to speak ironically of the "Marshal's National Revolution" as a patent medicine expected to cure every ill; he ridiculed the reactionary ideas of Charles Maurras and Pétain's other professional propagandists, with whom he never had much in common. He disliked the substitution of the title "French State", on official proclamations, coins and stamps, as much as he disliked the personal cult of the Marshal which became rampant and idiotic during his absence from power. He remained a disciple of Blanqui and of Sorel only so far as their technique of seizing and wielding political power was concerned. He wanted his "Revolution" to be confined to the political plane.

His removal from office in December, 1940, was effected in an oddly melodramatic and sensational manner, which reveals that Pétain was incorrigibly afraid of him. It was partly that he had served his immediate usefulness, partly that his open hostility to the "National Revolution" and to the cult of Pétainism had become tiresome: but more than anything it was fear lest he should wish to move further and faster along the path of economic collaboration than was necessary. He was very active—and mysteriously active—in Paris. "Laval worked day and night", writes an American observer: "I lived on the Rue Lascases and saw officials come and go at the Hotel Matignon as late as midnight."[1] The immediate occasion for dismissal was Hitler's plan to restore to France the ashes of Napoleon's son, the Duke of Reichstadt. The ceremony was to take place at the Invalides on Saturday, 14th December, 1940.[2] Only two days before did Abetz inform Laval, and extend Hitler's invitation to Marshal Pétain to attend the ceremony in Paris. Pétain refused to accept so abruptly discourteous an invitation. Abetz warned Laval of the "grave consequences" which might ensue if Pétain sustained his refusal. Laval hurried off to Vichy on 13th December, where he found Pétain apparently very willing to accept. Four hours later, at a hastily summoned meeting of the Council of Ministers, the Marshal, accompanied by Baudouin, asked each Minister to tender his signed resignation. When all had signed, Pétain announced that he accepted only those of M. Laval and M. Ripert. At his office, Laval found his telephone cut and the corridors crowded with police. His chauffeur was arrested and his car taken. Under strong police escort he was taken to Chateldon, where he found his home already heavily guarded by mobile forces. Here, too, the telephone had been cut, and Laval and his wife and daughter were placed under house-arrest. Next morning the Marshal broadcast a statement that he had dismissed

[1]Thomas Kernan, *Report on France* (1942), p. 243.

[2]According to *Gringoire* the idea was Benoist–Mechin's: cf. Jacques Lorraine, *Behind the Battle of France* (1943), pp. 72–8.

Laval for "reasons of internal policy". Admiral Darlan represented Pétain at the ceremony at the Invalides. On 16th December Laval was released. The Marshal summoned him to Vichy to tell him he knew nothing of all this and to offer him the choice of the Ministry of Agriculture or the Ministry of Industrial Production, both of which Laval refused. The view expressed by Abetz, that the whole thing had been staged by the Marshal's entourage, as a sort of "palace-revolution" to get Laval out of the way, seems most probable. "At the court of the Sultan of Vichy", said General de Gaulle, "a palace revolution has deposed the Grand Vizier." It was typical of the strange and inconsequential happenings which could take place in that odd menagerie of intriguers. The Marshal, old and in his dotage, was by nature very suspicious, and always found contact with Laval irksome. The evidence provided by Baudouin suggests that Alibert, Peyrouton, General Laure, Bouthillier, probably Darlan, and latterly Pierre-Étienne Flandin, were all in the plot to get rid of Laval;[1] and it was Flandin who was nominated Minister of Foreign Affairs in Laval's stead. It is also clear that it was the Germans who pressed, through Abetz, for the release of Laval, but who failed to get him reinstated in power.[2] A compromise was reached by making Admiral Darlan the heir-apparent of the Marshal, and by the promotion of Fernand de Brinon as the French "Ambassador in Paris".

The aim of Hitler during this period as regards France has since become clearly known from his

[1]Baudouin, *op. cit.*, pp. 284–98.

[2]*Ibid.*, pp. 293–7: *Le Procès Flandin*, 1947, pp. 169 and 182–5, where extracts from the relevant German documents are also quoted; and *Le Procès Pétain*, pp. 197–9, where Laval himself suggested the names of these "conspirators".

secret instructions produced at the Nuremberg Trials. In November, 1940, he wrote:

> The aim of my policy towards France is to co-operate with this country in the manner most effective for the future pursuit of the war against England. For the moment, France will have the role of a non-belligerent power; she will have to accept the military measures taken by Germany within her territory, particularly in the African colonies, and give them her support, as far as possible employing her own means of defence. The most pressing mission for the French is to protect, defensively and offensively, the French West African and Equatorial African possessions against England and against the movement of de Gaulle. From this initial mission of France may result complete participation in the war against England.[1]

A week after Laval's dismissal President Roosevelt appointed Admiral Leahy as Ambassador to France. Roosevelt wrote, "I had reason to believe that Marshal Pétain was not cognizant of all of the acts of his Vice-Premier and Minister for Foreign Affairs, M. Laval, in his relations with the Germans."[2] Leahy claims some share in the stiffening of Pétain's resistance to reinstating Laval in 1941, and in the rise of Admiral Darlan to greater power. The Darlan period seems to be the only phase of Vichy politics when American diplomacy exerted any strong influence, and it came to an end in 1942, when Leahy left and Laval returned.

[1]Quoted (in French version) in *Le Procès Flandin*, pp. 179f.

[2]Cf. Admiral W. D. Leahy, *I Was There* (1950), p. 517—a great revelation of how little the American Ambassador at Vichy understood the French scene. He was recalled by President Roosevelt in April, 1942, when Laval returned to power. His comment on "Black Peter", as he calls Laval, is characteristic. "He was a small man, swarthy-complexioned, careless in his personal appearance, but with a pleasing manner of speech. In a very frank discussion of his policies, Laval gave the impression of being fanatically devoted to his country, with a conviction that the interests of France were bound irrevocably with those of Germany (*ibid.*, p. 113). W. L. Langer, *op. cit.*, is the best full-scale examination of the motives and success of the United States policy towards Vichy.

It has been suggested both by Baudouin and by Flandin that just before Laval's removal from office he had been engaged in making a series of commitments with the Germans for the recovery of Chad and the Cameroons from the Free French: and that these agreements formed the real substance of Montoire.[1] It is said that Laval had agreed to French naval action against English ports in Sierra Leone and Gambia. It seems likely that the Germans asked for this, and it is inherently likely that Laval was prepared to play upon their hopes of getting it, and of getting French forces embroiled with British, in order to extract in return concrete concessions in metropolitan France—especially as regards the occupation-costs, the easing of the demarcation-line between the occupied and unoccupied zones, and the return of French prisoners of war. But one may be sure that the degree of active co-operation would have been kept to the minimum, that the time needed for adequate re-equipment of the French forces would have been prolonged and their needs fully emphasised, and that this seasoned bargainer would not in the end have given away more than he gained.[2]

The material bases of potential Vichy independence were already clear enough, and were fully appreciated by Laval: control of the French fleet, of the African colonies, of the "Armistice Army" of 100,000 men, and administrative control of the "unoccupied zone".

[1]Baudouin, *op. cit.*, pp. 280–3 and *Le Procès Flandin*, p. 178. Both men, of course, were Laval's personal enemies, so their statements must be treated with reserve. So too must the statements made by defence-counsel in *Le Procès Pétain* (e.g., p. 361) since their strategy was to whitewash Pétain by fixing the blame for as much as possible on Laval.

[2]Cf. *Ciano's Diplomatic Papers* (1948), p. 401 : Laval "stressed the psychological difficulty in the way of leading the French people to declare war on England at once ". Cf. W. L. Langer, *op. cit.*, p. 96.

These were the four legs on which Vichy's bargaining position rested; and so long as Laval could keep these free from German control then he had some cards to play in his quest for easing occupation-costs and the release of French prisoners of war. But he did need chances to play his game of political poker with the Germans—hence Montoire, and hence his frequent visits to Paris, and hence his constant lip-service to German aspirations for French co-operation against England and to the prospect of a total German victory. He was certainly not stupid enough to miss the point that after the Battle of Britain Hitler would be more than ever ready to join in the game of poker too: and as always Laval had boundless confidence in his own superior skill in any such battle of wits, which was the only kind of battle he relished.

The position was complicated, so far as the colonies were concerned, by secret negotiations which were conducted, from the end of September onwards, between Marshal Pétain and the British Government. Professor Rougier had been entrusted with a secret mission to London to reach a *modus vivendi* between Vichy and Britain. In October he met Mr. Churchill, Lord Halifax and Sir Philip Strang, and claimed that by the end of November an agreement had been reached. Vichy undertook thereby to defend all its colonial territories and fleet against German or Italian attack or infiltration, and not to make any unjustified attack against Britain. Britain undertook to give all possible help in French resistance to German or Italian pressure, and to restore eventually all French territories to French sovereignty. Meanwhile, if any part of the French Empire should spontaneously join the Gaullist camp, Britain would recognize it. On the basis of this "agreement", further arrangements were sought relating to French trade and the British blockade in the Mediterranean. Flandin continued negotiations to this end in January, 1941, with some success, and began parallel negotiations with the United States. There was a real fear, on the part of Pétain, Baudouin and others, that Laval's arrangements with the Germans might jeopardize or conflict with these precious new negotiations with Britain: and this doubtless helped to generate the concerted action which had ousted him from power the previous month.[1]

* * * * *

It is clear enough that Darlan and Flandin, in their own ways, pursued an essentially similar policy of trying to preserve room for their own independence between the opposing pressures of German demands and British necessities. Laval's chief indictment of their policy is that they carried it out less successfully than he himself would have done had he remained in power, with the result that they extracted less advantage from the Germans; and that by appearing to depart from the spirit of Montoire they discouraged the Germans from pursuing a policy of bargaining at all. "A little band of men void of any political experience or political principle, real sorcerer's apprentices, then began to play their little game of internal politics without realizing that it would be our country as a

[1]See Baudouin, *op. cit.*, pp. 256–7, 282; *Le Procès Flandin*, pp. 172–5; Winston S. Churchill, *The Second World War*, Vol. II, pp. 450–1; Mr. Churchill's statement in the House of Commons on 12 June, 1945; the White Paper published by the British Government on 1 August, 1945 (Cmd. 6662) and the full account in Louis Rougier, *Mission secrète à Londres*, revised edition printed in Belgium, 1947—a highly tendentious but very useful book.

whole which would have to pay, our prisoners and our finances, and that finally our remaining shred of liberty, which we were trying so hard to preserve, would be destroyed by their crazy and childish undertaking."[1] Instead of concessions, Laval's fall was followed by German tightening of the barrier between the occupied and unoccupied zones, and by increase of the pressure on the French administration generally.

Vichy entered a new phase of increasing *attentisme* —of lukewarm "wait-and-see" policy—which was to end only in April, 1942, when Laval once more returned to power. Flandin stayed in office only until February, 1941, when he was replaced as Minister of Foreign Affairs by Admiral Darlan.

Laval went again into retirement, living mostly in Paris and at Chateldon. His homing instinct was always strong, and he knew how to bide his time. What he did most of the time until his fateful return to power in 1942 is not known, but there are a few sidelights. He possessed a fine Russian *moujik* coat which Stalin had given him on his visit to Moscow. He amused himself by wearing it at Chateldon, and frightened his notary who happened to call at that moment.[2] Six months after his retirement began, Hitler launched his attack on Russia: and six months after that, Japan launched hers against Pearl Harbour. The whole war assumed an entirely different character. The role which Vichy France could play in world affairs was completely changed. It was a world war, with gigantic forces mobilized on each side. These forces, moreover, were piling up for a new trial of strength in western

[1] *The Unpublished Diary*, p. 95.

[2] Jacques Baraduc, *Dans la Cellule de Pierre Laval*, p. 75.

Europe. There was constant talk of the western allies opening a "Second Front" in the west: and that meant—could only mean—that metropolitan France, and probably also her North African territories, would again become a battlefield. Hitler was building defences along his "Atlantic Wall", in the occupied coastal zone. The French people seemed to be shut in a prison, with every danger that the onslaught which would liberate them might also bring them to the very brink of destruction.

One can well imagine the relish with which Laval watched the odds piling up against the Germans and Italians, and his impatience with the ineptitude of Darlan in failing to exploit their embarrassments and losses for the benefit of Vichy and of France. There were still two million French prisoners of war languishing in German prison-camps: the pick of French manhood, swept up into the armies of 1940 only to be kept away from their homes for four long years. There was still the artificial and hampering partition of France into two zones, still the crushing occupation-costs to be paid, for the privilege of keeping German troops on French soil. The problem of precisely why Laval sought to return to power in 1942 remains a crucial one for the understanding of the whole psychology of the man. Here he was safely in retirement, out of the firing-line, covered with an alibi of dismissal for all that Vichy might do meantime, and the odds were plainly turning increasingly in favour of an allied victory. During the liberation of France, could he not have emerged snugly from Chateldon, smuggled himself and most of his fortune across the Atlantic, and one day died peacefully in his bed? The Free French had, of course, a ready answer: he wanted, if not a German victory, at least a stalemate peace, for therein lay his best hope of survival. But let us examine both his behaviour and his own explanation for his return, before accepting this glib solution.

His own story is that in March, 1942, it was arranged for him to see Goering secretly at the Quai d'Orsay. Goering impressed upon him that any hope of collaboration was at an end, that the German treatment of France would soon worsen, and that in the event of German victory the terms of peace would be harsh. Laval reported the conversation to Marshal Pétain, who urged him to concert policy with Darlan. Darlan invited Laval to return to office, but he refused. "All the members of my family, without exception, begged me not to return to power."[1] It was indeed a thankless task, which it is difficult to believe anyone would have undertaken without strong promptings of self-esteem, forcing him to believe that he could handle the situation more skilfully than anyone else. It may well be supposed that the astute Goering planted the idea, despite his apparent discouragement of Laval, calculating that Laval's reaction would be to seize this opportunity to regain power for himself. There is evidence in Dr. Goebbels's *Diary* that he, at least, welcomed Laval's return in April, 1942: his words strike the authentic note of the Nazi attitude towards Laval. "The situation in Vichy", he writes on 15th April, "has now been clarified enough to show that in all likelihood Laval will enter the government in a few days as Prime Minister. This is a tremendous advantage for us, and for that reason it is

[1]*The Unpublished Diary*, p. 99; *Le Procès Pétain*, pp. 200–1.

causing alarm in London and in Washington. In any case, France under Laval, even though he is personally unsympathetic, is far more acceptable than a France of *attentisme*, with which you never know where you are." Three days later, he writes, "Speculation in London and Washington concerning the appointment of Laval continues. He is developing into the most sensational and mysterious personality of present-day international politics." And another three days after, he adds, "We could hardly find a better man than Laval for our policies. . . . We shall probably have to pay him something if he fulfils the hopes we place in him. But first it is for him to show what he can do."[1]

What were these "hopes" that the Nazis placed in him? It was to give them greater security than the passive policy of Darlan had given them on their vulnerable western wall, for with the German armies bogged in Russia the growing threat of a "Second Front" had to be taken seriously. It was to give Germany greater French collaboration, especially in the industrial sphere. Her heavy military losses combined with sustained allied bombing had seriously affected her industrial needs; and the only source of skilled industrial labour in any quantity was France. So larger numbers of French workers must somehow be induced or forced to go and work in German factories. It was, finally, to undertake both these tasks and yet subdue popular resistance, which was now assuming real military and economic importance inside France.

It was probably, in the circumstances, asking the

[1] *The Goebbels Diaries* (1948), pp. 122, 125, 129.

impossible. It might have been possible to get security by ferocious repression, as it might have been possible to get greater collaboration by concession: but it was not possible to pursue both aims at once. Yet it was the knowledge that necessity compelled Germany to seek both ends at once which was Laval's strength—it gave him a good bargaining position, such as he had been trying to build up for himself in 1940. Now the opportunity was thrown into his lap, and it proved irresistible. Marshal Pétain—under heavy pressure and persuasion from Laval and perhaps also from Germany—agreed to take him back into power in April. It seems to have revived in Italy the anxieties which had previously been aroused by Montoire. "Laval is at the head of the Government in France," wrote Count Ciano on 15th April, 1942. "Here are the results of long German labour, concerning which we have been kept entirely in the dark. Only after it was over did the German representative in Paris inform our Ambassador of what had happened, yet the matter concerns us directly. What promises have been made to the French in order to reach this conclusion? At whose expense? We shall see. For the moment it is hard to predict anything. But one thing is certain: Laval does not represent France, and if the Germans think they can conquer French hearts through him, they are mistaken, very much mistaken, again." Three days later he adds, "The Laval Government is formed. It is a Government of under-secretaries and unknowns. It practically remains a Pétain-Darlan government. Thus France prepares for all three eventualities: a British victory, de Gaulle; a German victory, Laval; a compromise, Pétain. If only all this does not end to our disadvantage."[1]

The position, both internationally and internally, offered precisely those elements of equilibrium which most appealed to Laval's ingenuity. All was not well between the Axis partners, so again France might hold Italy at bay by winning Germany's favour as against Italian claims. The alignment of British, Russian and United States power against Germany would produce for Germany just those urgent problems and material difficulties which France, properly led, might actively exploit to win concessions and advantages. Internally, there was a sharp conflict between the camp of the *attentistes*, centring on Vichy and led by Pétain, Darlan, Maurras and their colleagues, and the camp of the collaborationists, centring on occupied Paris and led by Déat, Doriot and the extremists. Laval, flitting between the two and agreeing completely with neither, could carve for himself a unique position of personal control over the main operative forces in French politics. The image of the man in the middle of the see-saw floated before his eyes again. But meantime, German pressure was stepped up, and the first ordeal was to cope with Gauleiter Sauckel, who had just been appointed to supervise the supply of French man-power for German economic needs.

[1]*Ciano's Diary*, pp. 457–8. In conversations with Ciano at the end of the month Ribbentrop even felt it necessary to reassure him, at great length, of German suspicions of Laval. Ciano noted, at the time, that "The Laval Government came into being without the knowledge of Berlin, against Berlin's wishes, not to say in outright opposition to Berlin, which would have preferred to keep Laval as a card in reserve for some time still." (*Ciano's Diplomatic Papers*, pp. 482f.). These renewed suspicions between the Axis partners are some measure of Laval's success in at least his immediate manoeuvres.

"The biggest brute that I've ever seen", was Laval's verdict later on Sauckel. Laval said to him, on one occasion, "You are the envoy of General de Gaulle." He clicked his heels and barked, "No, of Chancellor Hitler." "Ah", said Laval, "I thought you were the envoy of General de Gaulle—for the organization of the *Maquis*."[1] Laval had a fainting fit during his first interview with Sauckel, which was violent and lasted several hours. German labour demands, as successively pressed through Sauckel, were indeed drastic: 150,000 skilled workers by the middle of October. There is little doubt that it was Laval who seized on the device of linking supply of workers with release of prisoners, and who invented the famous scheme of *la relève*, which he launched in June, 1942. It was an ingenious device, intended to hoodwink Frenchmen by persuading them that they could work for Germany without feeling that they were being traitors to their country, because in exchange prisoners would be sent home to their families. The impression given at first was that the exchange was to be on a fifty-fifty basis of one prisoner for one worker, and doubtless this was what Laval was aiming at. But in August he had to admit publicly that only 50,000 prisoners would be released in return for 150,000 workers, and that workers meant "skilled engineering and metal workers". Further, no prisoners would be released until a large number of workers had actually arrived in Germany. It turned out to be a worse bargain than it had at first appeared. By the end of September only some 5,000 prisoners—the most aged and most ill—had returned, but 17,000 workers had

[1]Jacques Baraduc, *op. cit.*, p. 82.

gone. The swindle became obvious, and despite extensions of the time-limit, further inducements and a mixture of seduction and blackmail, the scheme collapsed. A census of labour was taken, and the regional Labour Commissioners in France were given quotas of workers to provide by a certain date. By early 1943 even this system gave way to simple labour-conscription, and in February all young men of twenty-one, twenty-two and twenty-three were called up for two years' compulsory labour in agriculture or industry. Germany demanded 250,000 workers in the first quarter of 1943, and another 220,000 in the second quarter. It meant mass deportations, and even so only 390,000 were sent to Germany in the first six months of 1943, of whom little more than half were skilled workers. With every sort of official and unofficial connivance the young men evaded conscription, and by simple desertion the ranks of the men of the *Maquis* were swelled with large numbers. In this way, resistance became more bitter and more massive, whilst economic collaboration remained less than Germany had hoped. The *relève*, of course, was popular with those families who did recover their menfolk: but it soon bred disillusionment when its terms became known, and to this mood of disillusion the deportations added bitter hostility.

"I struggled to obtain better terms", was Laval's defence later, "but it was impossible and I decided that the return of 50,000 Frenchmen was better than nothing at all. . . . My purpose was to obtain volunteers in order to stop the Germans from drafting French workers. . . . The whole purpose of my policy at this point was to create an atmosphere of artificial confidence among the German representatives whom I wished to convince that we were doing our best." He secured postponement of application of Sauckel's decree, instituting forced labour for all, by his own law of September, 1942, which was much less drastic: all occupied countries, except France, suffered from Sauckel's decree. "The only possible way of handling the Germans", believed Laval, "and of gaining precious time was to draft texts to exhibit to them but which no one had any intention of applying." The intervention of the Vichy administration had the effect of slowing down the drafts, when conscription was applied, and it tried to avoid some of the worst hardships. "As a last-minute measure", adds Laval, "we persuaded the Germans to exempt rail-workers, miners, policemen, prison officials, and other civil servants. We were able to write in the names of tens of thousands of young Frenchmen on the lists of civil servants and thus save them from deportation: rarely have the enlistments in the police and the penitentiary services reached such heights!"[1]

By April, 1943, the Germans seem to have been satisfied that, after one year of power, Laval had served their purposes better than they would have been served without him: one of the most difficult things for him to explain away in his defence. In that month there was an attempt to remove him once more from power, and Hitler himself intervened with Pétain to prevent Laval's dismissal. "I feel I should on this occasion let you know", wrote Hitler, "that since our interview at Montoire, M. Laval has devoted himself, not without success, to giving relations

[1]*The Unpublished Diary*, pp. 126–31; *Le Procès Pétain*, pp. 205–6, and 212–13.

between France and the Axis Powers a new basis which is advantageous to all parties. . . . On his part President Laval, since you, a year ago, called him to power, has devoted himself anew to collaboration with the Axis Powers; has given the French problem an orientation which takes account of the real facts of the problem, and which aims at supporting in an appropriate manner the Axis Powers and Europe against bolshevism and the western plutocracies allied with it."[1] He warned Pétain against a repetition of the events of December, 1940. By December, 1943, there was talk of another plot to remove Laval, by promulgating new constitutional laws, and this time it was Ribbentrop who wrote a long and typically rude letter to Pétain.[2] He pressed that Laval be commissioned to form a new ministry guaranteeing collaboration: and the result was the introduction of the extremist collaborators in January and February, 1944.

During the second half of 1943, German demands increased and their coercive measures increased in proportion. Laval claims that he still devised new means of obstruction, whilst keeping up an appearance of reluctant collaboration. He played off the Sauckel Labour Organization against both Speer's Armaments Organization and Backe's Agricultural Organization, which were also competing for French man-power. Bichelonne, his Minister of Labour, hit upon the idea of getting ten thousand French factories

[1]The full text, in French, is given in *Le Procès du Maréchal Pétain, Textes officiels du requisitoire et des plaidoiries* (published in Montreal, 1946), Annexe XII.

[2]The full text is given in *ibid.*, pp. 273–7, and Pétain's evasive reply *to Hitler* (not Ribbentrop) in *ibid.*, Annexe XV.

classed by the Germans as "S" factories whose workers could not be drafted. He attached French officials to the German labour-recruiting offices, to cause delays. Laval even personally dodged meeting Sauckel in Paris, to gain a few hours of time. By the end of July, 1944, 341,500 workers had gone to Germany, many thousands of whom gained leave to return to their families and then failed to return to Germany; and 110,000 prisoners had been returned to France. Would blank resistance—accompanied by ruthless German mass-deportations on a still larger scale and with no release of prisoners—have been a better result? As usual, Laval leaves out of account the moral gains of a united French resistance to the enemy, an uncompromising refusal to sup with the devil, even with a long spoon. But is he not, perhaps, substantially right in his estimate of the material gains which he won? At least he has the testimony of Sauckel in his favour: "All his efforts appeared to be bent towards gaining political advantages for France. . . . It is no longer possible to avoid the suspicion that Laval is taking advantage of these difficulties because he, just as everyone in this country appears to do, completely misunderstands the military and domestic situation of the Reich. Some allusions made by him make it clear that he believes he can now substitute France in Italy's place."[1] So wrote Sauckel to his Führer in August, 1943. Even he had begun to see the cloven hoof: and by November, 1943, the formerly enthusiastic Dr. Goebbels was writing: "Rather disagreeable developments are observable

[1]Sauckel's Report to Hitler from the German Archives in Berlin, printed in *The Unpublished Diary*, Appendix V.

in France. Laval keeps hesitating. It's not quite clear whether he is delaying from apathy or intrigue."[1]

* * * * *

But meanwhile certain other events had revolutionized the whole position of the Vichy Government, and these form the background to this period. In November, 1942, there had taken place the successful Anglo-American landings in French North Africa; the desertion of Vichy by Admiral Darlan, then the latest *Dauphin* of Pétain, and his assassination; the occupation by Hitler of the whole of metropolitan France; and the scuttling of the French ships by their own sailors at Toulon.[2] In one swoop all the foundations of Vichy independence had been swept away—even the small "Armistice Army" was dissolved by the Germans. Only the waning prestige of the ageing Marshal and the cunning manoeuvres of Pierre Laval held the ramshackle regime together at all. From then until D-Day, the task for Vichy was essentially one of playing for time. It had to resist the ever more desperate pressure of Germany, to do all it could to soften the impending blows which France must suffer from an allied invasion of her soil, and to delude the Germans as best it might into a false sense of semi-security in the west. When the allied landings took place Hitler offered Laval a military alliance. He and Pétain refused, but Hitler summoned Laval to Munich, to meet him and Ciano. Ciano's account of the meeting is most revealing:

[1] *The Goebbels Diaries*, p. 421.

[2] In his evidence at the trial of Pétain Laval made the neat point, in his own defence, that had the Germans thought they could get him to deliver up the fleet to them they would never have risked its scuttling itself in this way: an important and neglected point; cf. *Le Procès Pétain*, p. 210.

> A conference with Laval is almost superfluous, because he will be told nothing, or almost nothing, of what has been decided. Laval, with his white tie and middle-class peasant attire, is very much out of place in the great salon among so many uniforms. He tries to speak in a familiar tone about his journey and his long sleep in the car, but his words are unheeded. Hitler treats him with frigid courtesy. The conversation is brief. The Führer is the first to speak and asks pointedly if France is in a position to assure us landing points in Tunisia. Laval, like a good Frenchman, would like to discuss it and take advantage of the occasion to obtain concessions from Italy. I do not have time to interrupt, because Hitler, with the firmest decision, declares that he does not intend at this time to take up a discussion of Italian claims, which are more than modest. Laval cannot take upon himself the responsibility of yielding Tunis and Bizerta to the Axis, and he himself advises that he should be faced with a fait accompli; in short, we should draw up a note for Vichy in which it is stated what the Axis has decided to do. The poor man could not even imagine the fait accompli which the Germans were to place before him. Not a word was said to Laval about the impending action —the orders to occupy France were being given while he was smoking his cigarette and conversing with various people in the next room. Von Ribbentrop told me that Laval would be informed only the next morning at eight o'clock, that because of information received during the night Hitler had been obliged to proceed to the total occupation of the country. Laval owes it to me that a communiqué was not published which, even though it was not stated in so many words, gave the impression that Laval had given his approval to all the measures decided by the Axis. And yet the words loyalty and honour are always on the lips of our dear Germans![1]

Laval's own account throws a different light on Ciano's "failure" to interrupt. "At this point," he wrote, "Count Ciano intervened in the conversation, claiming bases for the Italian Air Force in the region

[1]*Ciano's Diary*, pp. 522–3.

of Constantine, to which I replied sharply. We had a violent altercation." The jackals were even then snarling at one another and lying about it afterwards.

The chief significance of this sequence of events in November, 1942, and the collapse of the material props of Vichy's power, is that they left Laval with only his own wits to rely on. As he wrote later, "I had no weapons that I could use against the Germans when they harried our land, nothing with which to fight them but my intelligence and strength of will. There were forty million Frenchmen to be protected and preserved. Could I hesitate an instant to employ words and phrases which bound nobody but myself when I knew that such words and phrases would help and might even save my country?"[1] If the bargains he was able to drive were less good than they might have been or than he expected them to be—at least they were also less good than the Germans had hoped for, as the evidence of Sauckel and of Goebbels shows.

Throughout the whole of this final period of power he met with increasing hostility from the more ardent collaborationists of Paris—Marcel Déat, Philippe Henriot, Jean Luchaire and the rest. After the total occupation of France in November, 1942, the collaborationist forces tended to get an ever tighter grip on Vichy, despite the resistance maintained by Pétain and by Laval himself. The Germans, too, were inconsistent in their policy towards their *protégé*. They could have made things as easy as possible for him, letting him consolidate his power and making some gesture of concessions which would have enabled him to pose as the man who could get better terms from the

[1] *The Unpublished Diary*, pp. 150–1.

Germans. Or they could have openly terrorized France into submission by starvation and bloodshed. The logical result of their welcome of his reinstallation was that they should make his regime as successful as could be, extracting economic advantages from the pacification of the country. But in practice they alternated between both policies. The mass execution of hostages whenever a German soldier was killed by resisters, which had begun under Darlan, now occurred even more frequently. Support was given to the attacks of the collaborationists on Laval. Had he not been able to offset these by pointing to the even more virulent attacks made upon him by French resisters and by the British, his reputation with the Germans would have declined faster. Goebbels appears to have seen the inconsistencies of the German attitude, for in December, 1942, he wrote: "In Paris, Doriot has again sharply criticised Laval. His speech teemed with insults against the French Premier. I think we shall have to gag Doriot sooner or later, as he is beginning to be quite a problem."[1] On the other hand, Ciano noted at this same period how useful was Laval's unpopularity in France when he was trying to convince the Germans of his usefulness and devotion to them. "He said one clever thing, that for him it is difficult to govern France, since everywhere he turns he hears people call out: 'Laval au poteau.' "[2] His collaborationist critics in Paris were, indeed, far more of a trouble to him than his Gaullist critics at home or abroad: though on one occasion at least, in 1941, Gaullist "criticism" took the concrete form of an attack

[1] *The Goebbels Diaries*, p. 176.
[2] *Ciano's Diary*, p. 537.

on his life from which he narrowly escaped. And he was able to use even his collaborationist enemies in the end, in his spirited defence in 1945: did their attacks not prove that he had been positively obstructing collaboration with the Germans?

The methods by which Laval contrived to keep his head above water by balancing between the *attentistes* of Vichy and the collaborationists of Paris are well illustrated by the complicated story of the Legions and Militias. In 1940 the Pétainists formed a *Légion française des combattants*, as a kind of ex-servicemen's association to support the Marshal's regime. Later the Tricolour Legion was formed, to absorb the keenest members of the Pétainist body: and within that in turn was formed the *Service d'ordre légionnaire*, with Joseph Darnand at its head. Meanwhile Jacques Doriot, an ardent collaborationist, had formed an Anti-Bolshevik Legion to fight against communism at home and on the Russian front, and in November, 1942, Darnand and others formed an "African Phalanx" to resist Anglo-American action in North Africa. The number of such para-military organizations became indeed legion, and the precise relations between them hopelessly involved. But gradually a few broad tendencies appeared. Each new legion that was formed was designed to absorb, and partially to replace, a rival body which had proved lukewarm or intractable; and Laval was constantly contriving to offset collaborationist legions with new legions controlled by himself or his henchmen, which would in the end co-ordinate and control the extremist bodies. In January, 1943, the Tricolour Legion was formally dissolved, but its *Service d'ordre* was placed under Laval personally and was merged into a new "National Militia". The members of these various bodies became something of a stage-army, mustered and passed on from one formation to another until they ended up—perhaps some 10,000 strong—as the National Militia controlled militarily by Joseph Darnand and politically by Laval. By constantly seeking a symmetrical balance between the bodies in the two zones, by unifying them and inserting his nominees such as Raymond Lachal or Joseph Darnand in the key positions, he succeeded in outwitting the manoeuvres of the collaborationists and keeping some grip on these dangerous movements. It was a *tour de force* of subtle and well-timed tactical moves.[1]

Faced, correspondingly, with a constant clamour for the formation of a *parti unique*, to form the basis of a real single-party State in France, Laval followed the opposite manoeuvre of preserving disintegration. He was greatly helped by the strong individualist tendencies of even the French fascists; each insisted on the desirability of a single-party formation to consummate the "National Revolution", but also insisted that his own particular group must be the core of such a party. He managed to keep the quarrels and divisions between Déat, Doriot, Luchaire and the rest active enough to prevent any danger of such a political merger. By nature, habit and instinct something of a lone wolf in politics, Laval had reason to fear the fusion of so many elements into one movement: and he did much to prevent it.

[1]See *The Times*, 18th August, 1942, 3rd February, 1943, and 22nd April, 1944 for articles analysing these formations; and D. M. Pickles, *France between the Republics* (1947), pp. 45–6; *Le Procès Pétain*, pp. 216–18.

Encroachment of the collaborationists on his power came only during the first six months of 1944. The Vichy regime was in its death-throes, amidst open civil war throughout the countryside. Its basis of even semi-independence gone, organized and militant resistance reaching a new height of intensity and ferocity, the prospect of armed invasion by the western allies looming ever nearer above the horizon, the whole regime lapsed into a phase of open terror. It was the inevitable "reign of terror" which has accompanied most French revolutions—the "red fool-fury of the Seine" in full spate. The collaborationists were in this period forced upon Pétain and Laval by German pressure, following Ribbentrop's letter, and out of sheer panic lest the resistance forces should give too much help to the invaders. It marked the abandonment of the German experiment with Laval, and the final recognition that he had failed to perform his double task of increasing collaboration whilst subduing resistance. The thug Joseph Darnand accumulated one power after another until, like Himmler in Germany, he held virtual power of life or death over every person in France. Already the key man in the various "legions" and para-military formations into which Laval had sought to co-ordinate rival movements, he became in 1944 "Secretary-General for the Maintenance of Order". He controlled the police and food supplies. Philippe Henriot of *Gringoire* became Secretary of State for Information and Propaganda. Marcel Déat became Minister of Labour and "Secretary of State for National Solidarity". This team of extremist collaborators, more utterly trustworthy than ever Laval had been because their very lives depended on delaying an allied victory, were Rundstedt's auxiliaries in his plans for the defence of the west. At last, and only at last, had Vichy become an authentic "quisling" government, performing completely the tasks allotted to it by the Germans. The Gestapo in effect ruled France, using the remnants of the Vichy administration as a very threadbare cloak for their terrorism. What did Laval do now?

* * * * *

It was here, at the very last stage, that he made his greatest mistake. Faced with this invasion of the collaborationists which preceded the invasion of the allies, he should—and still could—have washed his hands of Vichy. The tight-rope act which he had for so long contrived to perform between Germany and France, between *attentisme* and collaboration, between Paris and Vichy, was no longer possible. He claims that he believed he could still serve as some sort of barrier to the extremists but regretted it later.[1] If this was so, it was a serious miscalculation for a realist, because it was they who now controlled the levers of power at Vichy. Yet, it can be argued, he at least prevented an open declaration of war upon the allies, and as late as D-Day, when he read a message over the radio, the collaborationists drew up a manifesto with some four hundred signatures protesting to Hitler against his attitude.

Whatever his plans between January and June, 1944, he seems in August to have devised a characteristic scheme which only the course of events frustrated. On 9th August, 1944, still formally

[1]Cf. *Le Procès Pétain*, pp. 213–18.

Premier of France, he went to Paris and rallied to his support the eighty-seven mayors of Paris and the members of the Departmental Council of the Seine. He brought Édouard Herriot, formerly President of the Chamber of Deputies, to Paris and tried to convoke the National Assembly. He urged the Germans not to defend Paris. This last desperate manoeuvre has never received the attention it deserves. Its implications are fantastic. It means that even now, with all his past crashing about his ears, he really believed that he might still find a lever with which to prise himself free. He was aware of the reluctance of the allied Powers to recognize fully the Provisional Government of General de Gaulle.[1] He knew that its basis was in essence revolutionary. He was prepared to maintain, as he consistently did at his trial, that the Vichy regime had been quite legitimately created by the famous vote of the National Assembly in July, 1940. He now conceived that if he could summon it again he could serve two vital ends: he could re-establish a constitutional authority which it might be difficult for the allies to refuse to recognize, and once recognized this authority would implicitly throw a mantle of legality and legitimacy over the whole of the Vichy regime. It was a conception both bold and impudent, and it is a revelation of the ingenuity and astuteness of Laval that he should have made this attempt even in this very last ditch.[2]

He was frustrated by a combination of circumstances, and events moved too fast for even him to

[1]See below, p. 203. It was October, 1944, before the Provisional Government was given full and formal recognition by the Allies.

[2]The story of this attempt has been described in the extremely pro-Laval work of Maurice Privat, *Pierre Laval, cet inconnu* (1948), pp. 209–29.

exploit them. Déat and Darnand fled to Germany, and the collapse of the collaborationists left the necessary vacuum. But on 17th August he was arrested by the Germans and taken to Belfort, and thence to Germany. In September all his property in the Clermont-Ferrand region was confiscated by the State. On 20th October he was sentenced to death, in his absence, by a court at Marseilles. It was de Gaulle, and not Laval, who won allied recognition.

This amazing manoeuvre is in line with his return to power in April, 1942, and with his clinging to power after January, 1944. His behaviour on all three occasions cannot be simply dismissed, as it so often is, by the explanation that he lusted for power and high office, nor merely as a desire to save his own skin, though it might be argued that in 1942, and even in 1944, he felt more secure in power than out of it. But he could certainly not have pinned any hopes on German victory or even survival in 1944, and his defence would have been infinitely stronger had he been able to plead that he had refused to share power with the extreme collaborators in 1944. Had personal survival and timely preparation of an alibi been his chief considerations, he would scarcely have shouldered responsibility in the period just before D-Day.

The only thesis which adequately accounts for his behaviour on these three occasions is that he believed that by remaining in power he could carry out to the bitter end his original policy of serving as an obstruction to German domination and exploitation of France. None can know what mixture of motives, what medley of fears and calculations, govern a politician's conduct at such crises. But it is evident that he cared more for consistency of policy—and by his whole tough, peasant nature he instinctively clung to a policy which he had once adopted—than is commonly allowed. It is difficult to believe that any man who had not a deep inner conviction of his ultimate rightness of choice could have endured the long gruelling ordeal of the examination and trial which he was now to experience, or that he could have put up, against the heaviest odds, so remarkably vigorous and convincing a defence. If we dismiss Laval as a mere opportunist, a time-server, a mean trickster and a lickspittle politician of the lowest order, we miss his whole significance and fail to explain his conduct. It is only by crediting him with a sincere belief in at least most of what he professed at his trial that we can make sense of his previous actions at all. And it is this hidden source of strength, this fervour of confidence in what he had done, that explains the vigour and effectiveness of his defence, and the moral dignity of the way that he died.

But meanwhile he had more immediate physical hardships to endure. Along with his wife and his chauffeur, Boudot, who was devoted to him, he was successively transported by the Germans from Sigmaringen to Wielflingen, and thence to Wangen. Not least of the dangers was the threat—imminent in November, 1944—that he would fall into the hands of the Russians. At Wielflingen he was kept in a farmhouse. Watching a herd of deer being hunted, he noticed that two of them bringing up the rear retreated backwards, face to the enemy, in order to protect the others. "Like myself," he mused, with a smile: "Only I'm not sure of escaping from the hunters." At Wangen, tired of successive moves and faced with the desire of the Germans to take him to the famous Bavarian redoubt, he went on strike and refused to go any farther. The Gestapo officer in charge was at a loss, could get no order by telephone from Berlin, so let Laval wander into a nearby village. There he found himself surrounded, and recognized, by a group of released French prisoners of war. Laval chatted to them, explained what he had been trying to do. They included a school-teacher from Aubervilliers. It was almost as if he were back in Aubervilliers—they all insisted on shaking hands with *M. le Président*.

The Germans kept him in Germany and then in Italy until the spring of the next year. He was eventually released at Bolzano by a German commander, and allowed to make his way to the Swiss frontier. There he spent the last week of April, trying to gain admission to either Switzerland or Liechtenstein. It was reported that he was trying only to get permission to cross Switzerland into France, to place himself before French justice; and contrariwise that he was desperately seeking to avoid falling into the hands of the advancing French troops.[1] From this point onwards, events are obscured by a mass of contradictory rumours. But at the end of April he somehow persuaded two *Luftwaffe* non-commissioned officers to pilot him, in a Junkers 88, and at the beginning of May he arrived mysteriously and sensationally at

[1]According to *Daily Mail* (30th April, 1944) and *Daily Telegraph* (1st May, 1944) he wanted to reach France; according to *Daily Express* (1st May) and *New York Times* (3rd May) he did not. This kind of contradiction is almost constant at this time.

Barcelona. His wife and two former French collaborators accompanied him. Thus began perhaps the most remarkable phase of his whole career, which serves as a semi-comic preface to the final tragic act: it may be called the Spanish interlude.

The civil governor of Barcelona fed him and his wife in the aerodrome buffet. General Franco, as he was urged to do by Mr. Norman Armour, the United States Ambassador in Madrid, ordered that Laval should either leave the country at once or be interned. He chose internment, declaring that he would surrender only to a commission representing the allied nations. He and his wife were accordingly interned in the fortress of Monjuich, on the hilltop near Barcelona, where—as he later put it—the Spaniards "stuffed them with food"; although according to persistent rumours it was he who bought lavishly from the local Ritz Hotel and mounted up vast bills which he never paid, leaving the Spanish Government in the end to foot them all.

His position in Spain soon became the focus of a protracted, highly complex and obscure series of negotiations between the allied nations, and between them and Spain. His aim would seem, clearly enough, to have been the indefinite prolongation of this situation. He succeeded in prolonging it for three whole months. As the first of the major "collaborators" to be cornered, he raised many awkward problems. Was he a "war criminal" within the meaning of the term then being evolved for the purposes of international trials? Or was he a "traitor to France", and so the "private property" of France, to be tried only by a national court? Or was he a "political refugee", in the older sense of the words, and so entitled to some asylum in a neutral country such as Spain? The French Provisional Government seems to have favoured the view that he was a French traitor, and both the British and the United States Governments wished to have as little to do with him as possible. On the other hand, General Franco seemed more willing to hand him over to an allied authority than to France, for by so doing he would avoid the admission that Spain must surrender refugees from other countries. Gradually, however, he came to see the value of Laval as a possible bargaining-card, and there were persistent reports that he was trying to "trade" Laval for Señor Juan Negrin, the Spanish Republican leader then in France, or to win the right to demand the corresponding extradition by France of other Spanish Republican refugees.[1] The Spanish Foreign Minister, Lequerica, announced on 7th May that extradition was impossible because diplomatic relations had not been established between the two countries.[2] Laval became an acute international problem by merely continuing to exist. By the time that the French Government was more willing to seek an escape from this dilemma by letting Laval be handed over to Britain or to the United States, either as intermediaries for her or as agents for the allied Powers, these countries were far from anxious to assume responsibility for him. Meanwhile Laval seems to have used some pressure on General Franco, in the form of a threat to reveal various diplomatic conversations between him and Germany during the

[1]*Manchester Guardian*, 29th May, 1944.
[2]*Evening Standard*, 7th May.

Vichy regime which would embarrass Franco at a time when he was seeking more congenial relations with the Allies. This blackmail worked, to the extent that Franco showed for a time little anxiety to hasten Laval's departure.

In mid-May it was reported that various proposals were being considered. Perhaps he could be taken to a French port in a British warship? Or brought out via Gibraltar? Or sent into Andorra, which was policed by the French? It was reported that he had actually sailed in a British warship, but this later proved untrue. By the end of May deadlock had been reached. On 25th May the French Consultative Assembly was demanding a formal breach of relations with Spain because of her attitude to Laval. On 30th May General de Gaulle's Minister in Madrid, whose frail physique had been heavily taxed by the delicate negotiations, died of a heart attack. A few days later it was reported from Madrid that Laval had decided to give himself up to France. "I must follow Pétain's example", he said. The Spaniards issued a *communiqué* declaring that Spain "would agree to hand over Laval to France if he abandoned his right to remain in Spain"—and the last phrase seemed to betoken no intention of extraditing him.[1] By mid-June it was rumoured that a French plane had been sent to fetch him, but that at the last minute he had refused to enter it, and was still living at Monjuich in luxury and splendour.

His position during the second half of June was the subject for a still more exuberant crop of contradictory reports. According to the *Daily Express* he was cheerful,

[1]*Le Populaire*, 4th June, 1944.

tanned and nearly ten pounds heavier: according to the *Daily Telegraph* of the next day he had been ill for three days, was pale, and had lost weight.[1] The French press screamed itself hoarse about the lobsters and champagne upon which Laval, by reports, gorged every day. According to the *Daily Express* a week later, he was happily knitting himself a pullover; the *Evening Standard* the next day described the "winter woollies" he was knitting.[2] What was clear enough was that he was pulling the wool over the eyes of the world.

At the end of June the Spanish Government, at a full Council of Ministers specially summoned by General Franco, was reported to have decided that unless Britain or the United States demanded him, which they had hitherto consistently refused to do, he would remain in Spain. It seemed unlikely, despite previous reports, that France had even demanded extradition, because political prisoners had been expressly excluded from the extradition treaty between the two countries.[3] It was in the course of July that his position suddenly deteriorated, but nothing less than a change of the Spanish Foreign Minister effected this deterioration. Señor Lequerica, who had been on friendly terms with Laval and may indeed have wished to avoid unpleasant personal revelations, was replaced by Señor Artajo, who was on more friendly terms with M. Bidault, the French Foreign Minister. Strained relations between France and Spain were considerably eased by this change, and Spanish policy in general showed some anxiety to get

[1]*Daily Express*, 15th June; *Daily Telegraph*, 16th June.
[2]*Daily Express*, 23rd June; *Evening Standard*, 24th June.
[3]*Daily Mail*, 30th June.

on better terms with the allies. The Labour Party victory in the British general election was interpreted as likely to bring a hardening of allied attitude towards Spain unless she softened her own. Whatever the decisive reason, the Spaniards decided to send him packing on the same plane and in the same conditions as those in which he had arrived three months before, and they issued the delicious statement that "Pierre Laval was formally invited by the Spanish Government to leave their territory and, agreeing to this invitation, the ex-Premier of the French Government left this morning. . . ."[1] The French consul at Barcelona was duly informed. Laval and his wife were put into the plane with the two *Luftwaffe* pilots, and the plane took off from the aerodrome near Barcelona at 4.30 p.m. on 30th July. It was forced back because of engine trouble and the party had to spend yet another night in Spain. But the next morning it took off again, heading for Austria, and it landed at Horsching, near Linz, with its petrol almost exhausted. Its actual objective had been Salzburg.

At Horsching they were taken into custody by the United States Army Air Force, and were sent under escort to the headquarters of the French Zone, near Innsbruck. Thence they were sent by Dakota plane to Le Bourget on the evening of 1st August, under French escort. Amongst his baggage brought from Spain was a symbolic item: two wooden cases of bottles of Vichy water.

At Le Bourget he was formally arrested. Elaborate precautions had to be taken to prevent his falling

[1] *Daily Telegraph*, 1st August.

into the hands of armed bands of resisters who had vowed to waylay him. Amidst crowds shouting "Death to Laval!" he was rushed by the back streets to Fresnes prison, where a cell had been held ready for so long to receive him. Here he was lodged for the duration of his trial. Already at Monjuich he had been busy preparing the main lines of his defence, and at an early stage in the Spanish interlude he seems to have accepted as inevitable his eventual appearance before a French court. Any hopes of a more lenient trial before an international court which he may earlier have cherished soon disappeared. His main concern had been to prevent his sudden violent assassination, and to ensure that he should have an opportunity of appearing in a court. Not only did he succeed in this aim, but by his last great triumph in manipulating the balance between Spanish pride and French anger, between allied hesitation and French vacillation, he had gained a precious three months of time—and of life. Events had played into his hands, as so often before: and he proved that he had lost none of his old *expertise* in exploiting them.

How far had he willingly returned to France? How far had Spain given him up only under concerted pressure from France, Britain and the United States? These are still difficult questions to answer precisely. In the end he was forced to go, and in the interval both Britain and France had certainly backed French demands that he should be expelled.[1] Yet there had equally been moments when he seems to have independently decided to go—perhaps because he wearied

[1]Cf. statement by Mr. Joseph C. Grew, U.S. Acting Secretary of State, reported in *New York Times*, 1st June, 1944; and by Mr. Richard Law in House of Commons, on 6th June, 1944.

of the strain and anxiety, perhaps because he felt he would strengthen his position by forestalling the inevitable.[1] Certainly he accepted trial in the end with more than resignation, remarking, "If Pétain can face the music, so can I." The trial of Marshal Pétain was in process in July and August, and it was timely for him to reappear on the scene then, as his evidence in the trial shows. The problem of determining the willingness and the compulsion which lie behind his return to France is not easy: and it is the problem of his whole career. How far did he really dominate and determine the course of events? How far is it merely that his skill in exploiting pre-determined events makes the whole story appear afterwards as one controlled by his scheming?

* * * * *

The *premier interrogatoire*, the pre-trial hearing with which political trials begin in French law, took place on 23rd August. Questioned about his private fortune, Laval explained that *Radio-Lyon* had prospered only when he replaced the soldier, who was at the head of it when he took over, by a technician. Was there a parable of Vichy in this? The enquiry, bound by its nature and by the varied nature of the charges to be a lengthy and tedious affair, dragged on for the rest of August and into September. Josée was approached by a powerful newspaper with the offer that if her father would give certain revelations about an eminent personality of the Third Republic, his trial would be slowed down. Laval indignantly rejected the offer.

[1]On 6th June Laval wrote to General de Chambrun, of his son-in-law's family, expressing his wish to return to France. The General strongly advised him to stay where he was. On 17th June Señor Lequerica said that Laval had, in a letter, offered to surrender to the French (*Sunday Times*, 17th June).

All the time he conducted his defence with amazing agility and vigour, trapping his judges into stupid positions, quick with repartee to pompous questions. And in his cell he wrote frantically to get his thoughts and recollections, as well as his defence, on to paper. Never did his remarkable memory serve him better. "*Dieu, que vous êtes intelligent!*" exclaimed one of his judges involuntarily. "It is you, *Monsieur le Juge*", retorted Laval, "who are intelligent. . . . You are a great magistrate. . . . You have always been a great magistrate. . . . At Riom . . ." In September the High Court abruptly broke off the *instruction*. M. le Président Beteille, who had had some rough handling from Laval, opportunely went off on his holidays, thoughtfully taking with him the keys of the locked-up *dossier* of the accusation.

When, on 4th October, the actual hearing of the case began, it opened with Laval alone conducting his defence. The President read a letter from Laval's counsel protesting that they could not take part because the *instruction* was still incomplete. They pointed out that the trial was blatantly being hustled so as to get it through before the elections, and they refused to take any share in such a procedure. Not that Laval needed their professional services, for he conducted his own defence with consummate skill. It was he alone who kept his head, and who sometimes put his accusers, judges and jury in the box. His jokes raised laughs in the court. The charges, badly and loosely drafted, gave him ample opportunity to make the prosecution look stupid. The judges got rattled, the jurymen hurled insults across the courtroom, the whole place fell increasingly into an uproar. His counsel appeared on the second day, but after the third day Laval also refused to appear, and the spectacle of a trial conducted with neither accused nor counsel for the defence in court became utterly farcical.[1]

The blatant misconduct of the trial and Laval's skill as a debater won him reluctant sympathy and admiration from large sections of French opinion. The whole affair aroused shame and disgust, and reflected great discredit on the Provisional Government of General de Gaulle. Here is the verdict of one who cannot be charged with any undue sympathy or liking for Laval, and it is an accurately just verdict.

> The conduct of the President of the High Court and of the chief counsel for the prosecution, *le procureur général* Mornet, had already been much criticized. Both were old. The former was weak and clumsy, the latter abusive and over-bearing. Moreover, about both there clung suspicions, if not of sympathy with, at least of acquiescence in, the policy of Vichy. If they did not show up well morally during the occupation, or professionally during the trial of Pétain, words fail to describe their lamentable exhibition of their shortcomings at the trial of Laval. The President was entirely unable to control the behaviour either of the jury or of the public. Uproar and consequent suspension of sittings succeeded each other so frequently that it was doubtful, almost from the beginning of the trial, whether it would be able to proceed. Indeed, if it had not been for the imminence of the general elections and the anxiety of everyone to see the Laval case settled before they took place, there might well have been a deferment. As it was, the trial was concluded in the absence of the accused who, after three days, refused to appear again before the Court, on the grounds that neither judges nor jury were prepared to give him a fair hearing. His counsel were in agreement with him and refused to plead.[2]

[1]For full report, see *Le Procès Laval: compte rendu sténographique* (1946).
[2]D. M. Pickles, *op. cit.*, p. 194.

An intervention by M. Teitgen, Minister of Justice, which was mingled with excuses and apologies for the behaviour of the judges, was of no avail: Laval and his counsel still refused to appear and to plead.[1] Even the express wish of General de Gaulle that the counsel at least should plead was refused. The judicial authorities were at a loss to know what to do. "*Pauvres types! pauvres types!*" muttered Laval: "When I'm not there they no longer know what to do!" He went on reading his detective-story in his cell: it was set in Auvergne. There was only one thing the Court could do, to save its face. They passed sentence of death, on the basis of what had already been heard of the evidence. It was passed on 9th October, 1945. His counsel interviewed Léon Blum and General de Gaulle, while Laval in his cell took to reading François Mauriac's *Vie de Jésus*.[2] Blum expressed his utter disapproval of the conduct of the trial—"a scandal and a mistake". General de Gaulle, just before the interview, announced at a press conference that the verdict on Laval could not be reconsidered. The execution was fixed for eight o'clock on the morning of 15th October. The general elections for the new Assembly were to be held on the 21st.

On the appointed morning his counsel and the prison authorities came to his cell. They found that Laval had swallowed a phial of cyanide, which he had kept hidden in the cell for a long time. The prison doctors revived him enough for the execution to take place at eleven o'clock: but as he could not stand the twelve kilometres journey to Montrouge, he had to

[1] J. Baraduc, *op. cit.*, pp. 143–6.

[2] He also expressed great admiration for the Koran: can it be that he visualized mediation between two different Heavens?

be executed in the prison-yard at Fresnes. The Germans had used it, too, for some of their executions. He accepted absolution from the priest. He dressed, carefully choosing his last white silk tie and donning his tricolour scarf. Leaning on the arms of his counsel he walked slowly from his cell.

As the shots of the firing-squad rang out the other prisoners did not, like the war-time crowds, shout "*Laval au poteau!*" They did not, like the jurymen at his trial, rejoice at "a dozen bullets in his hide". They shouted "*Assassins!*" and "*Vive Laval!*" There was administrative muddle about the disposal of his body. Even in the grave he was haunted by the contradictory orders and confused counter-orders of the administrators of the Republic. His last hours had been spent drafting a *critique* of the sentence of death, but it was left unfinished.[1] He quite literally argued and defended himself to the last breath.

* * * * *

One of Marshal Pétain's defence-counsel at his trial, Maître Isorni, summarized aptly the contrast between the policy of Pétain and the policy of General de Gaulle and the Resistance. "The policy of the Marshall was as follows: to safeguard, defend, acquire, material advantages, but often at the price of moral concessions. The Resistance had a contrary conception: it sought in no way to avoid immediate sacrifices. In continuing the struggle it saw, first of all, moral advantages."[2] This desire to minimize material sacrifices and secure material gains was what Pétain and

[1] It is printed in Baraduc, *op. cit.*, pp. 213–26.
[2] *Le Procès Pétain*, p. 365.

Laval had most consistently in common. Pétain saw, with an old man's eyes and a defeatist spirit, the possible ruin of France's material existence as one consequence of her defeat. Laval, always prone to neglect or under-rate moral values, believed that to talk of preserving France's honour at the expense of her material existence was the worst treason possible to France. Like most pacifists and realists, he could never understand why others regarded it as more honourable to gain ends by brute force and violence than to gain them by bargaining and guile. If one could create, in the minds of the Germans, a Sorelian "myth" that Vichy stood for solid collaboration with Germany, would that not be a much more effective way of gaining advantages than by open sabotage, assassination and "resistance" which would inevitably attract ever more savage reprisals and losses, which the French would be powerless to avoid? He saw no sense in fighting Germany with weapons in which she was utterly superior. But might he not prove that he was even a bigger double-crosser than Hitler?

It was exclusively on the matcrial advantages he had helped to gain for France, the material sacrifices he had helped to avoid, that Laval rested his defence. And with him, as with Marshal Pétain, it will remain the only possible historical justification for their behaviour. Alone of the defeated countries of Europe, France did not become the helpless victim of Gestapo rule until the last six months before D-Day, when the team of collaborationists virtually ruled the whole country. Alone of the defeated countries, her women never suffered compulsory labour-service. Alone of the defeated countries, she gained some return for the deportations of workers to German factories. These gains, in terms of human hardship and suffering, are not slight; and they would have been impossible without the existence of a Vichy Government which could bargain with the Germans and draw some gains from their difficulties and setbacks. On the other hand, the worst legacy of Vichy was the bitterness and fratricidal strife which haunted French national life for three or four years after liberation. The dramatic conflict between the two contrasting attitudes which Maître Isorni indicated split asunder French public opinion and national life, and the wounds have not completely healed yet. That is the great moral loss which Laval bequeathed to France. It was a loss which made his own death imperative and inevitable: though the bungling of his enemies and his own agile mind combined to rob even his execution of any moral grandeur, save that which derived from his own physical courage in the face of inexorable punishment.

The essence of Gaullism's case against Laval, as against the whole *raison d'être* of the Vichy Government, was summed up by the Gaullist Minister of Justice, M. Teitgen. "I know very well all that M. Laval has done for his country; but the whole problem is to know whether, in order to defend the body of France, it was necessary to lose her soul."[1] This is a problem which Laval never would or could have understood. He could not see any sense in talking of saving a soul if the body was lost. His whole temperament and philosophy of life were utterly alien to any such notion. He was of the earth, earthy, and never

[1]Quoted in Baraduc, *op. cit.*, p. 145.

was a man less other-worldly. He rejoiced in good farms, rich soil, fat cattle, good food and wine, happy family life. He believed in the intrinsic goodness of human happiness. He believed, and it was the most completely consistent belief of his whole life and his career as a public man, that it is the first duty of a government to preserve the material basis of national life, and to foster the material prosperity of the country. He was that rare phenomenon—a consistent materialist. The notion of national honour, so much on the lips of French politicians and soldiers, seemed to him nonsense if divorced from the concrete problems of increasing human welfare and happiness. Likewise he was poles apart from the argument that "the only thing defeat allows you to save is dignity".[1] He had no objection to loss of dignity if it won (or prevented the loss of) material assets. It was repudiation of what they regarded as a debased conception of government which the Gaullists meant to demonstrate when they executed Laval. Yet by their manner of demonstrating it, they failed. It was Laval who won in the end. One commentator, at the time of his death, expressed it in these ominous words: "Laval's trial is unpardonable, because it made the French doubt the reality of French justice, so that none of our institutions, henceforth, will be immune from that disillusioned scepticism which finally renders a people ungovernable and drives men straight to anarchy. . . . Now the harm is done. French justice is discredited. Laval has won the last round and completed the demoralization of the country."[2]

[1]Charles-Roux, *op. cit.*, p. 294.
[2]Quoted D. M. Pickles, *op. cit.*, p. 195.

The antithesis to the ideas and political habits represented by Laval is "Gaullism", as it evolved during the four years of German occupation. In turning to this other side of the coin, we can perhaps discover the purport of other forces which have moulded present-day France. From the death of a *politique* we turn to the genesis of a *mystique*: and these two conceptions, as Charles Péguy has taught, are the eternal basic conceptions of French national life.

Charles de Gaulle

The depth, the singularity, the self-sufficiency of a man made for great deeds are not popular except in critical times. Although those in contact with him are conscious of a superiority which compels respect, he is seldom liked. . . . What possesses him is not, to be sure, the passion for rank and honours, which is only careerism, but beyond doubt the hope of playing a great role in great events. (*Charles de Gaulle*)

I preserved the impression, in contact with this very tall, phlegmatic man: "Here is the Constable of France." (*Winston S. Churchill*)

Quand les militaires se mettent à faire la guerre, ils ne la gagnent pas toujours, mais quand ils se mêlent de faire de la politique, c'est un catastrophe. (*Pierre Laval*)

IF PIERRE LAVAL, the man of Auvergne, was a son of the French countryside, Charles de Gaulle is a man of the French towns. He was born and spent his youth in Lille, a town of heavy industry, blazing furnaces and clanging steel works. Auvergne belongs to central and southern France, Lille to the extreme north—on the very borders between France and Belgium, so often crossed by the invader. He was born on 22nd November, 1890. His family was one of historians and writers, his home one of study and learning. It was an ardent Roman Catholic family, whose life centred on the old cathedral of Lille. His father was a professor of philosophy and of French literature at the Jesuit College in the Rue de Vaugirard in Paris. In this highly urban and cultured environment, in an atmosphere of religion and learning that belonged to old France, the boy was brought up. Herein Charles-André-Joseph-Marie de Gaulle, to give him his full name, acquired a taste for academic philosophy which never left him. He was encouraged to see ideas and principles as absolutes, and the values he was taught to cherish were those of the traditional culture of France. He is reputed, as a little boy, to have been *parfaitement diable*, *horriblement diable*, in the household. He and his brothers and sisters played tricks on everyone in the house. He became notorious in the family for his passion for tin soldiers, and for the *blitzkrieg* which he loved to wage with his troops against those of his brothers. He later said that before he was twelve he had decided that it would be his destiny to guide the nation through crisis; and that he had accordingly drawn up for himself a programme of study in history and philosophy.[1] But it appears to have been his earliest ambition to become a soldier: an ambition not uncommon among the old Catholic families of France under the Republic. It was a time when the Dreyfus Affair was splitting France in half, and ranging the forces of Catholicism, militarism and nationalism against the Republican forces of anti-clericalism, radicalism and socialism. The good Catholic who wished to serve his country as a good Frenchman tended to shun politics, and to seek an outlet for his energies in the armed forces, the colonial administration or the Church.

By the time he was twenty-one Charles de Gaulle passed his preliminary examinations successfully and

[1]Gordon Wright, *The Reshaping of French Democracy*, p. 42.

entered the famous Military Academy of Saint-Cyr, the best training ground for officers of the infantry and cavalry. It had been founded by Napoleon I, and in it the cult of Bonapartist generalship was kept alive. De Gaulle studied the Napoleonic epic closely, and acquired a profound admiration for it. He was already an unusually tall lad, and acquired the nickname of *la grande asperge*. But he had all the persistence of asparagus as well as its height, and having set his heart on being a soldier he worked hard enough to become a first-rate soldier. He revealed tremendous energy and sense of discipline. He passed his leaving examination with enough brilliance to be given the privilege of choosing which regiment he would join. He chose the 33rd Infantry Regiment and joined it at Arras in 1913. Its commanding officer was Colonel Philippe Pétain.

The newly commissioned second-lieutenant was moved around from one garrison to another, which gave him a broader view of France. He was only twenty-three when the First World War began, and he had just been promoted to the rank of lieutenant the year before. His recollection and picture of the outbreak of war are very different from Laval's. They show how utterly he belonged to the "other France", knowing nothing of the France with which Laval was familiar even in 1914. In his study of *France and Her Army* he later gave this description:

> France, then, had only to draw her sword to unite all her children in a common fervour, animating not only the mass but the individual. Inspired by patriotism, religious faith, hope, or hatred of the foe, he was both ready and willing to be torn from home and family. Theories, on the other hand, which had been considered

> to be potential obstacles to the war effort, vanished into thin air. Not one organized group raised its voice to condemn mobilization. Not one trade union thought for a moment of hindering it by strikes. In Parliament, not one vote was cast against the war estimates. . . . The suspects, whose names appeared on *Carnet B*, begged to be sent to the front.[1]

Colonel Pétain before long appointed the young officer to command of a company, and during the first two years of war—which were two of the most desperate fighting—de Gaulle showed his soldierly abilities in action. In August, 1914, in a violent action at Dinant, on the Meuse, he was severely injured. As soon as he had recovered he took part in the fighting at Mesnil-les-Hurles in Champagne, and here he was again wounded in March, 1915. In that year he was promoted to the rank of captain. Finally, he took part in the historic fighting around Verdun, in March, 1916, where Pétain was to gain eternal fame in French military history for his resolve, "They shall not pass." During the battle for the fort of Douaumont, in the mêlée of hand-to-hand fighting, he was thrown to the ground unconscious. He was picked up by a German patrol and taken to a nearby field-ambulance, where his wounds were given first-aid treatment. Then he was taken to a prison-camp hospital in Germany. When he had recovered he was interned, first at Friedberg and than at Ingolstadt, for the rest of the war. Five times he tried to escape, but each time he was recaptured within a few miles of the camp. His height made him too easily identifiable. Each attempt was followed by more severe punishments imposed upon him by the camp

[1]*France and Her Army* (Eng. trans., 1945), p. 90.

commandant. It was a gallant career thus abruptly interrupted. He had been mentioned three times in despatches. The solitude and tediousness of prison-camp life irked him terribly. He was compelled to spend two years and eight months in captivity until the armistice of November, 1918, secured his release. He returned home, weak and badly run-down, but at once reported for duty with his unit.[1] He also compiled his observations on the dissensions within Germany in her moment of defeat. It was called *La discorde chez l'ennemi*, and eventually appeared in 1924 as his first published work. He was anxious lest Germany should emerge from her defeat more unified, strong and aggressive than ever. But although his book was well received his warnings attracted little attention at the time.

He was meanwhile, however, raised to the rank of Commandant, and served for a while as professor of history at his old college of Saint-Cyr. In 1921 General Weygand was appointed to lead the French Military Mission to Poland, to aid her against the Bolsheviks. De Gaulle was taken as one of the officers on his staff, with the duty of liaison with Marshal Pilsudski. The Mission took part in the victory of Lublin, although it may be said that Pilsudski won it largely because he rejected Weygand's advice. De Gaulle duly returned to France having been again specially mentioned by Weygand, and with the Polish Cross of Saint Wenceslas as a decoration. There followed a long period of sick-leave; a course of lectures given

[1]According to Pertinax (*Les Fossoyeurs* (1943), Vol. I, p. 56), his promotion as a General was retarded because of an anonymous note in his dossier, accusing him of lacking experience because he had spent so long in a German prison camp!

at Saint-Cyr; and then, in 1922, a special course of training in strategy and tactics at the famous Parisian centre for the training of the General Staff, the *École de Guerre.*

Philippe Barrès tells a revealing story of de Gaulle at this time. The official doctrine of tactics taught at the *École de Guerre* rested on the assumption that the defence was stronger than the offence, and that "fire" had preponderance over "movement". The method of study was therefore *a priori*, and consisted in the minute study of a previously selected area for battle, in organizing its defence in great detail, with lines of fire and attack and retreat, and in then drawing the enemy on to this chosen pitch where his inevitable defeat had been so carefully prepared. It was a spider-and-fly conception, characteristic of the highly academic art of warfare which prevailed at this time. It was later to result in the conception of the Maginot Line. Charles de Gaulle rejected this doctrine and all its assumptions, remarking, "The enemy isn't more stupid than we are: he, too, will look for the most favourable battle-field." His masters at the School deprecated this originality and presumption. When it came to the tactical exercises at the end of the course, de Gaulle, commanding the "blue party", quietly tried out his own doctrines and ignored those he had been officially taught. He prepared no selected terrain, and preserved his freedom of movement. The exercise ended in the complete victory of the "blue party" and the discomfiture, personal as well as tactical, of his orthodox teachers, who penalized de Gaulle in his final examination. There was the inevitable fuss, which came at last to the ears of the

General in charge. It was Marshal Pétain. According to the story he was interested, and ordered de Gaulle to write a full account of what he had done; and as a result appointed de Gaulle *chargé de cours* at the *École de Guerre*.[1]

In 1925, at any rate, Marshal Pétain took de Gaulle on to the staff of the *Conseil Supérieur de la Guerre* in Paris. He was assigned the special task of studying the organization of the territory of France in time of war. He examined historically the defence of France's north-eastern frontiers, and at the end of 1925 published, in the *Revue militaire française*, an article which attracted considerable attention. He contended that fortification of her frontiers was for France a permanent military necessity. It was, paradoxically, welcomed by the champions of the idea of a Maginot Line, which was then under consideration. In 1927 he gave his three famous lectures at the *École de Guerre*, the first of which Marshal Pétain himself attended, and at which he introduced Captain de Gaulle with the words, "Listen to him attentively, for the day will come when France in gratitude will call for him."[2] He spoke on the role of leadership in war, and spoke provocatively. He later repeated the lectures to a wider audience at the Sorbonne. During these two years he had not only studied the basic military problems with which his name will always be associated in French history: he had studied and expounded them in a memorable manner which laid a foundation for his later reputation as a military expert of original and luminous mind. Throughout these years he had

[1]Philippe Barrès, *Charles de Gaulle* (1941), pp. 24–6.

[2]L. Nachin, *Charles de Gaulle, Général de France* (1944), p. 49.

served in the closest contact with Marshal Pétain, and acquired for the Marshal a tremendous admiration which led him to dedicate one of his books to him. His destiny seems, indeed, to have been closely bound up with the Marshal's at every crucial point.

In 1927 Pétain gave way to Weygand as commander-in-chief of the Army. Major de Gaulle was transferred to Trier (Trêves) where for the next two years he commanded the 19th Battalion of *Chasseurs à Pied*, in the French army of occupation in the Rhineland. He saw at close quarters both the deterioration in the French army and the early stirrings of German resurgence, and both confirmed his early conviction that Germany had not been defeated decisively in 1918. Speaking German well—for he had studied it in his prison-camp—he gained a solid grasp of the military position in the west. Then, suddenly, he was transplanted to a very different world. He was sent on a special governmental commission to the Levant. He went to Egypt, Iran, Iraq, Syria. In Aleppo, Damascus and Baghdad he spent two years attached to the military staffs of the Army of the Levant. He described the achievements of this remarkable army in his book *L'Armée du Levant.*

In 1931 he was recalled to France. The substance of his lectures was published as *Le fil de l'épee*, and the book was dedicated to Marshal Pétain. On his arrival he was raised to the rank of Lieutenant-Colonel and appointed to the secretariat of the *Conseil Supérieur de la Défense Nationale*. He held this important administrative post for some four years, and meanwhile he worked on his most famous book of all, *Vers l'armée de métier*, which appeared in 1934.

It was an eloquent plea for intense mechanization and for a professional army. It sold in France by the hundred and in Germany by the thousand. He tried to find politicians who would pay some heed to his arguments, since the highest ranks of the army seemed impervious to them. He found Paul Reynaud and Gaston Palewski. Reynaud voiced the arguments in the Chamber of Deputies, most notably in the budget-debate of 1935. He also embodied them in two publications of his own, *Le problème militaire français* and *Jeunesse, quelle France veux-tu?* The French General Staff not only resisted the arguments but ridiculed them. In Germany General Guderian, a military technician like de Gaulle, absorbed them and in 1938 advocated the lessons of them for German rearmament in his book *Achtung-Panzer!* M. Philippe Barrès found, as early as 1934, that both Hitler and Ribbentrop were familiar with the name and notions of Colonel de Gaulle as the best modern French expert in the art of war. But he was still almost unknown in France. It was a remarkable case of the prophet knowing no honour.[1]

His next book, *La France et son armée*, which appeared in 1938, was the occasion for a curious *contretemps* with Marshal Pétain. Invited by a publisher to produce a non-technical work for a wide public, he bethought himself of the notes and scripts which he had originally prepared in 1925 on the historic organization of France's northern defence-system, and which he had touched up from time to time in moments of leisure from military duties. He sought approval from his former chief for the publication of this work, all of

[1]Philippe Barrès, *op. cit.*, pp. 14–19.

which de Gaulle had written himself. He received an immediate refusal. Pétain claimed that the work was a product of the General Staff, and that the compiler of it could not be authorized to appropriate it for himself by publication. When de Gaulle protested, the Marshal agreed to publication provided that it was dedicated to himself and that he himself might write the dedication. De Gaulle rashly agreed, and then found that the text of the dedication prepared by Pétain implied that the author had more or less written it under dictation. He replaced it by a very respectful dedication which avoided this erroneous implication, but Pétain insisted, under threats of penalties, that his original text should appear in the second edition.[1] The story reveals both the incorrigible vanity which had by now beset the old Marshal, and the omens of a coming struggle which was to write such petty differences in vast letters on the pages of French history.

In 1936 came a brief return to the *École de Guerre*, and in the following year he was placed in command of the 507th Regiment of Tanks at Metz. Again in the Rhineland, where he stayed for the next two years, he could watch the feverish efforts at defensive rearmament on both sides of the river. It must have been a period almost as irksome as his years of captivity in the First World War. He knew that behind the new Siegfried Line, apparently so like the Maginot Line in its assumptions of static defence, there was being prepared a massive force of mechanized divisions, tanks and aircraft, which could reduce the Maginot

[1]The story is told in L. Nachin, *op. cit.*, pp. 91–3. The book was an immediate success; there is an English translation (1944) by F. L. Dash, with no dedication at all.

Line to absurdity. In England Winston Churchill was giving warnings against German rearmament.

In 1939, when the Second World War began, Colonel de Gaulle became commander of the brigade of tanks attached to the Fifth French Army in Lorraine. The war in Poland endorsed his worst fears. The German Panzer divisions swept through the country in a few weeks. The mechanization which Britain, with her invention of the tank in 1917, had begun, and which Charles de Gaulle, with his remarkably prophetic insight and independence of mind had foreseen and urged as the salvation of France, became for a time the chief cause of throwing both into mortal peril. It was the army of Germany which was the most modern in the world, and which—adopting the time-honoured technique of *blitzkrieg*—seemed about to dominate the whole of Europe.

The period of the "phoney war" gave him one last chance to try to awaken and convert his superiors. On 26th January, 1940, he drew up a memorandum for his superior officers and the government. It was a conclusive, incisive, irrefutable summary of his old but unheeded arguments for mechanization and freedom of movement. He sent a copy of it to Paul Reynaud and to Gaston Palewski, both of whom were at the moment embroiled in delicate hostilities with Édouard Daladier, the Prime Minister. It was little heeded. France still had only three light mechanized divisions dating from 1934, and four heavy armoured divisions, as against at least ten heavy armoured German divisions.

* * * * *

On 15th May General Giraud was transferred from the broken-down Netherlands front of the VII Army to the equally broken-down Meuse Front of the IX Army of General Corap. He found the IX Army confined within a huge triangle formed by the three great rivers of the Meuse (on the east), the Sambre (on the north-west) and the Aisne (on the south). The Germans, since 10th May, had blown a gap of some thirty-five miles on the Meuse near Sedan, and through this gap were pouring German forces of every description. Giraud rearranged some of his units, and at once withdrew Colonel de Gaulle from the Maginot Line zone in Lorraine, where he had been commanding his tank brigade, and made him Brigadier-General in charge of the new 4th Armoured Division. It was not the last time that the fortunes of Giraud and de Gaulle were to be linked. Giraud had the impression that he had three existing armoured divisions at his disposal, and drew up a plan for an immediate counter-attack to stem the German break-through. But all three divisions turned out to be mythical. These three were already sadly disorganized or too weary and exhausted to be immediately thrown back into the battle. The 4th, General de Gaulle's, existed largely on paper, but this did not deter de Gaulle from mustering what he could find. He added to its fighting power by every form of hasty improvisation such as armour-plating lorries, and threw it into the battle. Giraud's great counter-offensive turned out to be "a sortie by de Gaulle's half-formed division".

De Gaulle spent 15th and 16th May setting up his headquarters at Bruyères, five miles from Laon, collecting the miscellaneous and fragmentary units which were all he could be given, and surveying the terrain. It included some of the great historic battlefields of France and Britain—Crécy and Agincourt. On the morning of 17th he was ordered to attack the main line of the enemy advance. His light tanks moved forwards on the towns of Sissonne and Montcornet. They suffered heavy losses from anti-tank fire and were driven south to Agincourt. His heavy tanks crossed the canal at Chivres, captured the village, and surprised and destroyed a convoy of some thirty enemy trucks. Then dive-bombers came, and successive waves of them smashed at his tanks all afternoon. At 4.0 p.m. the Germans launched a strong counter-attack against the left flank of de Gaulle's division, but a regiment of reserves had just arrived: they were thrown straight into the battle, and the counter-attack was beaten back. His tanks withdrew over the canal that evening. It was a remarkable performance against such tremendous odds: and the balance-sheet was a hundred and fifty German prisoners taken and a good deal of enemy equipment destroyed, against a loss of ten heavy tanks and forty light ones. On 18th the Germans took Sissonne, but the line south of the canal was held. On 19th de Gaulle received orders from General Georges to move north through Laon and halt the German advance south of the Serre. His only reinforcements meantime were a few light-medium tanks with untrained crews which arrived during the night. He duly advanced on 19th.

The 4th Armoured Division advanced in two columns, the column of heavy tanks on the right to take Crécy, the column of light tanks on the left to take the bridge at Challandry. The Germans were strongly entrenched on the opposite bank of the Serre, and the bridges were blown up. For four hours the dive-bombers, unimpeded by any French planes, again smashed at the Division. By evening General Georges ordered de Gaulle to fall back so as not to pay too heavy a price. He withdrew south of Laon through the forest of Bruyères. The enemy pushed on to Laon, harassing de Gaulle's men from all sides. But the 4th Division broke free, and on 20th fell back behind the Aisne, in the south. It had attacked, inflicted damage, held up the enemy for three days. It had been unable to stem the main German advance, and so had little effect on the campaign as a whole. But de Gaulle had tried out his principles and methods, and his effort stood out as a brilliant exception to the handling of the other tank divisions.

The 4th Armoured Division was now withdrawn for reorganization, and was attached to the X Army stationed near the coast south of the Somme. Meanwhile reorganization was also taking place at a higher level. On 19th May the general command was taken out of the feeble hands of Gamelin and was given to General Weygand: he was seventy-three. Marshal Pétain came back from Spain, where he had served as French Ambassador, to become Vice-President of the Council of Ministers: he was eighty-four. On 26th May the first boatload of troops left from Dunkirk. On 29th May the entire 4th Armoured Division, now brought up to strength so as to include two battalions of light and two of heavy tanks, a rifle battalion, a regiment of motorized infantry and a colonial infantry regiment, was ordered to attack the German bridgehead at Abbeville. The Germans were dashing for the coast, and Abbeville was the key town on their route. De Gaulle's aim was to deprive the enemy of the bridgehead from which to launch a major offensive against the X Army: it was defensive in purpose. His attack began on the afternoon of the 30th May, less than a fortnight after his previous action at Laon. He tried three times on three successive days to establish a position of sufficient advantage to make the bridgehead untenable for the Germans. He suffered extremely heavy losses, both in men and material. He failed in his purpose, and had to retire exhausted. On 2nd June General Weygand mentioned de Gaulle in one of his despatches in these words, which must be taken as the official estimate of a confused and debatable enterprise. "An admirable, energetic and courageous leader. With his division he attacked the bridgehead at Abbeville which was strongly held by the enemy. He broke through German resistance, advanced almost nine miles inside the enemy lines, and captured hundreds of prisoners and a considerable amount of war *matériel.*" The judgment of Mr. Theodore Draper is harsh but just. "At best, de Gaulle's attack was merely an isolated interlude in the encirclement of the Allied armies of Belgium. It was apparently the strongest attack on the southern side of the gap, which is the best commentary on the other efforts."[1]

On the night of 6th June de Gaulle received an urgent message from Paul Reynaud, now Prime Minister. At 4.0 p.m. he arrived in Reynaud's office,

[1]Theodore Draper, *The Six Weeks' War* (1946), p. 207, to which I am indebted for the picture of the battles here given. Mr. Draper correlates the evidence for them from Major-General Aschenbrandt, *Militär-Wochenblatt* (10th July, 1942) and from Philippe Barrès's biography of de Gaulle.

to learn that he was to become Under-Secretary of State for War. "I want a strong, clear-minded man in the Cabinet", said Reynaud.[1] He wanted to be entrusted with the defence of Paris, but both Pétain and Weygand opposed the suggestion. With German forces closing in on Paris the government on 10th June left for Tours. But meanwhile, on 8th, de Gaulle had been despatched by Reynaud on special mission to London, accompanied by General Spears, to explore means of continuing the war. He saw Winston Churchill, who gave him the warmest encouragement for carrying on the fight.

He returned to Paris on 9th June, to find the Government on the point of leaving the capital. He hoped that the plan of retiring to the "Breton redoubt" might be followed. On 11th June, Churchill flew to meet Reynaud at the *Grand Quartier Général* near Briare. He records that he found at the rendezvous, "M. Reynaud, Marshal Pétain, General Weygand, the Air General Vuillemin, and some others, including the relatively junior General de Gaulle, who had just been appointed Under-Secretary for National Defence."[2] Churchill found France heading for military collapse, and returned to England next day. On 13th he flew to Tours, to meet Georges Mandel and Reynaud. "As we went down the crowded passage into the courtyard I saw General de Gaulle standing stolid and expressionless at the doorway. Greeting him, I said in a low tone, in French: *L'homme du destin.* He remained impassive."[3] The tussle continued within the French Government between those

[1]Count Alfred A. Hassenstein, *A Giant in the Age of Steel*, 1944, p. 37.
[2]Winston S. Churchill, *The Second World War*, Vol. II, p. 136.
[3]*Ibid.*, p. 162.

who wanted to ask for an armistice and those who wanted *la guerre à outrance*.

On 14th June, two days before the fateful cabinet-meeting at Bordeaux when Reynaud resigned, General de Gaulle again flew on special mission to London. His assignment was to explore with the British Government the means for transporting the French Government to North Africa, the transference to Britain of German *Luftwaffe* prisoners of war, and other similar urgent business. He arrived that night, and next morning he saw Mr. Anthony Eden, Sir Robert Vansittart, and M. Corbin. From these, and doubtless from previous discussions, there emerged the startling idea of "an indissoluble union" between France and Britain. Although for long known as "Churchill's offer of Union to France", it in fact originated mainly from General de Gaulle. There are two pieces of evidence of this. One is the evidence of Mr. Churchill himself:

> I was not the prime mover. I first heard of a definite plan at a luncheon at the Carlton Club on the 15th, at which were present Lord Halifax, M. Corbin, Sir Robert Vansittart, and one or two others. It was evident that there had been considerable discussion beforehand. On the 14th, Vansittart and Desmond Morton had met M. Monnet and M. Pleven (members of the French Economic Mission in London), and been joined by General de Gaulle, who had flown over to make arrangements for shipping to carry the French Government and as many French troops as possible to Africa. These gentlemen had evolved the outline of a declaration for a Franco-British Union with the object, apart from its general merits, of giving M. Reynaud some new fact of a vivid and stimulating nature with which to carry a majority of his Cabinet into the move to Africa and the continuance of the war.[1]

[1] *Ibid.*, p. 180.

The other is that provided by Dr. B. S. Townroe, who points out that private discussions of such a project had taken place in 1938 and 1939, and that lectures were given in Paris in the spring of 1940 by Lord De La Warr, Sir Duff Cooper, Lord Beveridge and others, in general support of such a union. He writes,

> Accordingly General de Gaulle, in May, 1940, found already in existence the outline of a plan, but asked M. Monnet to prepare a more detailed scheme. It is understood that at the request of Mr. Churchill an alternative scheme was prepared by Mr. L. S. Amery and Sir Arthur Salter. The whole question came to a head at a luncheon at the Carlton Club on Sunday, June 16th, when the two drafts were discussed. . . . M. Jean Monnet's proposals were for a *Union Franco-Britannique Indissoluble*, with one War Cabinet, one High Command and the two Parliaments formally united. The English draft was more modest, allowing for the pooling of financial resources, but leaving the political issues for further discussion, for fear of the probable reaction of the French Cabinet if the proposals went too far and too quickly. The General, however, was insistent on the French draft being accepted.[1]

There is still further supplementary evidence in the *Diaries* of Paul Baudouin, who describes the scheme as "Churchill's suggestion for which General de Gaulle had been working in London", and adds that M. Reynaud was "enthusiastic over it".[2] The offer which was eventually put formally before M. Reynaud as coming from the British Government was, in effect, based on the French draft prompted and supported by General de Gaulle. It was as follows:

[1]Letter to *The Spectator*, 8th October, 1948. It is not clear whether this Carlton Club luncheon (on 16th) is the same as the one to which Mr. Churchill refers (on 15th).

[2]*The Private Diaries of Paul Baudouin*, p. 116.

Declaration of Union

At this most fateful moment in the history of the modern world the Governments of the United Kingdom and of the French Republic make this declaration of indissoluble union and unyielding resolution in their common defence of justice and freedom against subjection to a system which reduces mankind to a life of robots and slaves.

The two Governments declare that France and Great Britain shall no longer be two nations, but one Franco-British Union.

The constitution of the Union will provide for joint organs of defence, foreign, financial, and economic policies.

Every citizen of France will enjoy immediately citizenship of Great Britain; every British subject will become a citizen of France.

Both countries will share responsibility for repair of the devastation of war, wherever it occurs in their territories, and the resources of both shall be equally, and as one, applied to that purpose.

During the war there shall be a single War Cabinet, and all the forces of Britain and France, whether on land, sea, or in the air, will be placed under its direction. It will govern from wherever it best can. The two Parliaments will be formally associated. The nations of the British Empire are already forming new armies. France will keep her available forces in the field, on the sea, and in the air. The Union appeals to the United States to fortify the economic resources of the Allies, and to bring her powerful material aid to the common cause.

The Union will concentrate its whole energy against the power of the enemy, no matter where the battle may be.

And thus we shall conquer.

Mr. Churchill describes his own first reaction to the scheme as "unfavourable". He found, with surprise, that a large section of opinion in his Cabinet was extremely enthusiastic. General de Gaulle pressed upon him again the urgent desirability of some such dramatic move. When the final draft had been approved by the British Cabinet, Mr. Churchill describes how "the General read it with an air of unwonted enthusiasm, and, as soon as contact with Bordeaux could be obtained, began to telephone it to M. Reynaud."[1]

It is both ironic and tragic that at that very moment Reynaud was engaged in securing agreement of the British Government to release France from her formal obligations not to make a separate peace. Britain agreed to his inquiring about the terms of an armistice with the strictest proviso that the French Fleet should forthwith sail to British harbours pending the negotiations. This reply, received on 16th June, threw Reynaud into dejection. At that moment the offer of Union came through. It acted like a tonic, delighted Reynaud and Mandel, and the Prime Minister set off to present both to President Lebrun. A telegram instructing the British Ambassador to delay or at least "suspend" the stiff reply about the conditions of releasing France from her obligations under the Anglo-French Agreement was sent off in the hope of giving the offer of Union a more favourable chance of acceptance. It reached the Ambassador only after Reynaud had set off to see Lebrun. Paul Baudouin records with great perplexity the confusion caused by the delivery and recall of the British replies about the armistice, which were re-delivered to the new French Government on 17th June, after Reynaud's resignation. He shows how the well-meant offer of Union served only, in the event, to obscure the British stipulations during the critical decisions about the conditions of an armistice which were reached by

[1]Winston S. Churchill, *op. cit.*, p. 184.

Reynaud and his successors on 16th and 17th.[1] Much hung on such trivialities: and it is Mr. Churchill's opinion that, "It is possible, even probable, that if our formal answer had been laid before them the majority would have accepted our primary conditions about sending their Fleet to Britain, or at least would have made some other suitable proposal and thus have freed them to open negotiations with the enemy, while reserving to themselves a final option of retirement to Africa, if the German conditions were too severe. But now there was a classic example of 'Order, counter-order, disorder.' "[2]

The French Prime Minister read the offer of Union twice to the Council of Ministers on 16th June, declaring himself strongly for it. It was at 5 o'clock in the afternoon, after a very long and tiring series of crises. "Without denying its importance," remarks Baudouin, "the Council considered that it bore no relation to the immediate problems that were calling for a settlement." Faced by insistence that they must ask the Germans for terms, Paul Reynaud resigned and asked the President to nominate Marshal Pétain in his stead. It is difficult to avoid Baudouin's cruel verdict that "in designating Marshal Pétain as his successor, M. Paul Reynaud joined the ranks of those who supported the request for an armistice."[3] The meeting ended at 7 o'clock, and

[1]Paul Baudouin, *op. cit.*, pp. 114–24; evidence of M. Charles-Roux in *Le Procès Pétain*, pp. 232f.

[2]Winston S. Churchill, *op. cit.*, p. 187.

[3]Paul Baudouin, *op. cit.*, p. 117. But cf. the interesting note on this point in Vincent Auriol, *Hier-Demain*, I, p. 67. Reynaud feared that the country would follow Pétain and Weygand if there were an open conflict with them, and insisted that it was MM. Jeanneney and Herriot who advised Lebrun that Pétain should properly be asked to form the new government. Herriot disputes this. So what?

the offer of Union had not even been seriously discussed, nor was it voted upon. "Fusion with a corpse", Pétain called it, for he believed, as did so many others, that in a few weeks Britain, too, would have to sue for an armistice. Very few people in France even heard that such an offer had been made, and no text of it was published there.

General de Gaulle landed by aeroplane at Bordeaux late on the evening of 16th June. He learned by radio that Reynaud had resigned and Marshal Pétain had taken his place, with General Weygand as Minister of War. He found negotiations for the armistice already in train. Next day the Marshal broadcast his famous announcement that the government had decided to end the struggle and to seek an armistice "between soldiers and in honour". Mr. Churchill immediately sent a personal message to Pétain and Weygand, and copies of it to President Lebrun and Admiral Darlan. He reiterated British anxieties about the fate of the French fleet. Lord Lloyd, Mr. A. V. Alexander and the First Sea Lord were sent to reinforce the British point of view in personal contacts with the new French Government. That night General Spears, British liaison-officer at the French G.H.Q., telephoned Mr. Churchill from Bordeaux expressing his anxiety about the safety of General de Gaulle, and proposing that he should leave France at once. "So that very morning", writes Churchill, "de Gaulle went to his office in Bordeaux, made a number of engagements for the afternoon, as a blind, and then drove to the airfield with his friend Spears to see him off. They shook hands and said good-bye, and as the plane began to move de Gaulle stepped in and slammed the door. The machine soared off into the air, while the French police and officials gaped. De Gaulle carried with him, in this small aeroplane, the honour of France."[1]

On 18th June the General gave his famous broadcast to the people of France. Rejecting both defeat and despair, he made the most momentous decision of his life. He placed himself at the head of a new movement and a new organization, to carry on the war alongside Great Britain. The soldier-technician became, overnight, the soldier-politician. Hitherto he had shunned all direct participation in politics, and had remained the specialist in modern warfare seeking to press his ideas directly upon the General Staff, and upon the Government through the mediation of politicians. Although always manifestly intrigued by the political implications of military strategy, he had been reluctant to admit that his views involved political issues, as in the circumstances they inevitably did. Even now, when he was making what was in fact a major political decision, he failed at first to realize that it was a political decision. He viewed it as the resolve of a soldier of France to continue the fight—a military and strategic decision which, though doubtless an act of insubordination and rebellion, was still in its essence a question of warfare. Only gradually did the full significance of his action become apparent, even to himself. On 18th June he spoke as a commanding-officer rallying his scattered troops.

> I, General de Gaulle, at present in London, invite French officers and soldiers who are on British territory,

[1]Winston S. Churchill, *op. cit.*, Vol. II, pp. 191–2.

or who shall come here, with or without their arms, I invite the engineers and specialised workers in the armaments industries who are on British territory or who shall come here, to get into touch with me.

The next day the tone was already changing. Referring to himself as *soldat et chef français*, he claimed to speak "in the name of France". By combination of the force of circumstances, the inexorable logic of events, and—it is clear enough—personal temperament, this note of political leadership was to become ever more authoritative and pronounced in the weeks ahead.

* * * * *

Before following Charles de Gaulle on the long and eventful journey which began when he jumped aboard the aeroplane as it left Bordeaux airfield, we may gain further insight into his character and personality by examining the main features of his military ideas as a technician. Just as the features of Pierre Laval, the technician in parliamentarism, repeated themselves on a larger screen in his major principles of policy, so those of Charles de Gaulle, the technician in mechanized warfare, have some bearing on de Gaulle the politician. They have, moreover, an intrinsic historical interest in themselves: though it is not proposed here to examine his military doctrines exhaustively and systematically for their own sake. Our concern is only with the ways in which human character and qualities of mind express themselves in choice of means no less than in choice of ends; and with how a choice of means may, to some extent, determine choice and achievement of ends.

The core of Charles de Gaulle's military creed is to

be found in his most famous work, *Vers l'armée de métier*, of 1934. It marks both the maturity and the synthesis of his previous thinking about military affairs, and it embodies his most significant contributions to the study of modern warfare. It combines, with a literary smoothness, his deductions from the study of both geography and history. He applies these deductions to the problem of French defence. Geographically, he sees France as well defended by natural barriers on all sides save at the vital point—her north-eastern frontier. Devoid of effective natural barriers to invasion, this sector of her defence invites attack. Here geography "organizes invasion" by several deeply-penetrating inroads, the valleys of the Meuse, Sambre, Escaut, Scarpe, Lys, where river, road and railway all conspire to serve and guide the invader. Successful invasion along any of these lines may lead to a decisive break-through. Historically, it is along these in-roads that France has always been invaded. But whereas historically it may have been relatively unimportant that Paris, the capital of France in every sense, is situated so vulnerably on the convergence of these inroads, it matters vitally now with modern means of rapid movement. Similarly, the concentration of essential heavy industries and mineral resources around this vulnerable area is a standing menace to French material security. Germany, on the other hand, is peculiarly well defended against attack from France, and her capital is conveniently remote. In short, he accepts and quotes Napoleon's dictum that "the policy of a State lies in its geography".

Given this permanent gap in her natural defences,

France has been driven to seek security by artificial means: by diplomacy, through alliances; by sea-power, through a strong navy and overseas bases; by military strength, through great fortifications and a national army. The only source of material security left to her in the modern world is a combination of fortifications with a powerful army and air-force: for France must be able to withstand the very first blows, the first shock of the modern *blitzkrieg*, if she is to stand at all. She has no protective margin of time, like her more fortunate neighbours of Great Britain and the United States. A sudden, overwhelming attack is made possible by the use of machines. It is mechanization of land, sea and air warfare which has made the traditional peril particularly acute for France to-day. It can be met only by the comparable use of machines. Only tanks and aeroplanes can effectively resist tanks and aeroplanes. This demands a high degree of expert and technical specialization, impossible in an amateur civilian army. The logic of the whole situation is that France needs, urgently and vitally, a professional, mechanized army.

Having built up, with sound academic learning and acute logical deduction, his case for the *armée de métier*, de Gaulle discusses its place in modern "total war", which involves in the long run all the material and human resources of nations. It is whole peoples which are involved, but since a whole population cannot be engaged in the first stages, there is special need for a kind of "shock-force" of highly skilled mechanized units, to gain enough time for the more massive reorientation of the whole nation.

He argues that the French genius anyhow does not

lie in mass-movements and mass-organization. The spirit of individualism and independence comes uppermost in Frenchmen, except in the last resort of extreme emergency. The military form most fitted to her national character is a selective, skilled organization, relying on the initiative and individual quality of its members rather than on the sheer weight of numbers. This is the one great advantage which France has in present conditions: her genius lends itself to that formation which is anyhow most desirable on technical grounds.

Getting down to the details of the structure and organization of such an army, he suggests that it needs 100,000 men; that it be completely mechanized and motorized, and operate on a combination of tanks, armoured cars and aviation. Its method of warfare will be one of rapid movement, enabling concentration of overwhelming striking-power at any given point of defence or attack. It must, of course, be a fully trained professional army of experts, a military *élite* so organized as to constitute a single striking weapon. It will consist largely of young men, for the qualities it calls for are those of youth—dash and mobility. After the age of 26 most of its members will be drafted to the reserve-lists. Although specialized in training, their knowledge of other specialisms in the army must be wide enough to make them intelligent specialists. Likewise their training, and the terrain of their training, must be as varied as possible. The soldier must be one of the best educated and most widely experienced of men. The almost lyrical enthusiasm with which Charles de Gaulle describes the selection and duties of the young soldier in his professional army recalls Plato's guardians and auxiliaries, and Sparta's disciplined bands. It has something in common—though for a very different end—with Hitler's *Ordensburgen*. The boy who loved tin soldiers and marshalled them for a *blitzkrieg* on his brother's toys has never completely ceased to exist.

Linked with this enthusiasm for the disciplined life of the military *élite* is de Gaulle's habit—more noticeable in *La France et son armée* than in *Vers l'armée de métier*—of suddenly embarking, amidst logical analysis and persuasive argument, upon a vivid picture of preparations for battle, or of a battle itself. It is as if his mind is suddenly confronted with a visual picture of how the whole machine will operate, and he builds up an imaginative film-sequence of the men and machines in action. It is a startling and curious trait, given rein so freely as to give an impression of a positive love of skilfully planned battle.[1] He clearly takes some pride in his literary capacity to depict such scenes, and it must have been a very effective lecturing device. It is significant of the sort of stimulus which arouses an otherwise cold and detached, somewhat academic, mind to verbal vivacity.

He ends his book with a chapter on leadership and command. It is the theme which he had dealt with in his lectures of 1927. He writes with the experience and authority of one who had exercised such command not only on the training-ground but in the actual field of battle. He traces how the evolution of weapons has brought with it a change in the methods,

[1] E.g., *Vers l'armée de métier* (1944 ed.), pp. 172–81; *France and her Army* (English ed., 1944), pp. 95–8.

and even in the functions, of generalship. In the First World War the commander in battle was removed from the scene, and compelled to study maps instead of inspiring his men on the spot. "Everything conspired to give generalship a remote, collective, anonymous character, forcing back genius and intuition into the shade." Because in modern warfare the human factor is so much subordinated to the mechanical, a new technical element enters into generalship. Yet the rapidity of the action once it has begun requires instantaneous decisions, wherein imaginative intuition and the natural genius for generalship will play an even greater part than before: and this is required at every rank of command, not only at the highest level. Once battle has begun, "the judgment, attitude and authority of the leaders depend above all on the intellectual and moral reflexes which they have acquired throughout their whole career." He adds a warning against subjection to routine and orthodoxy, and praise for the general of independent and original mind, who defies orthodoxy in the name of realism. His concern is with military politics—a plea for greater freedom for the innovator and heretic.

In the course of the argument he moves away from the particular problems of French defence to more general problems of modern national warfare, but only to return to them again. French policy demands the power to intervene at an early stage, to prevent her government's being presented with *faits accomplis*. Diplomatic alliances, designed to reinforce France's own security, call for readiness on her part to help to defend her allies. This advice, given in 1934, would have prevented the German occupation of the Rhineland, the *Anschluss*, Munich and Poland: it was one of the most profoundly prophetic parts of a remarkably prophetic book. It was lack of such a force, and lack of will to create and use such a force, which compelled France to submit to Hitler's series of preliminary aggressions which preceded and made possible the Second World War. He emphasizes that France "needs the army of her policy", and recurs to a theme which in his writings he continually approached but never elaborated: the relationship between the technique of warfare and the art of politics.

He emphasizes, too, a fact which plays a large part in all his arguments: that "our national existence has become that of an empire". His years in the Levant had brought home to him that France's military preparations, like her national policy as a whole, must be moulded in overseas and imperial terms. He thinks always of her overseas possessions, and clings to Lyautey's conception of France as a "nation of a hundred million souls". The role played by the overseas empire during the four years after 1940, both in the fate of Vichy and in the fate of the Free French, bore out his beliefs. So, too, after liberation, he was foremost in sponsoring the idea of the French Union. Charles de Gaulle is, in the Churchillian sense, an imperialist. Both in military and in political affairs he thinks on a world-wide scale and studies the large maps.

Vers l'armée de métier is so comprehensive a synthesis of all de Gaulle's essential concepts of military organization and politics that his other writings need be touched on only lightly. On the issue which, in his eventual career, was to prove most central—the relation between war and politics—his first publication throws some light. His study of *La discorde chez l'ennemi* was a clever semi-historical, semi-psychological examination of Germany in defeat. It falls into five parts: the disobedience of General von Kluck; the declaration of submarine warfare; relations with the Allies; the fall of Chancellor Bethmann-Hollweg; the downfall of the German people. He was concerned to draw from these facets of German experience certain inferences about the conduct of the war, the qualities desirable in leadership, the maintenance of popular morale, and the need to subordinate military strategy and the conduct of military operations to general national policy. It reveals a concern with, and a shrewd understanding of, German national characteristics and the danger of a German resurgence. His work of 1932, *Le fil de l'épée*, was—like the implicit ideas in his final chapter of *Vers l'armée de métier*—a criticism and even a condemnation of the personal qualities of the French High Command. It held before the professional soldier a new and more vigorous conception of his role, a more exacting definition of his duty, than the existing High Command required. It includes great homage to the qualities that make for a dictatorship—which many recalled after 1945. It was a summons to take stock, to reconsider the whole basis of soldierly life and functions: and it pointed to what was wrong (lassitude, conventionality and lack of enterprise) in the existing hierarchy. Yet it was dedicated to Marshal Pétain, and in effect gave such impetus to all who wanted to strengthen the military preparedness of France, that it could scarcely be openly condemned by authority.[1]

The arguments of his memorandum of 26th January, 1940, to the French High Command, bring all these long-pondered ideas to a single point, and relate them to the immediate concrete situation of France at war. It is a truly remarkable document, showing both the consistency and persistency of Charles de Gaulle. He gives a warning against a swift surprise attack by Germany, a repetition of the blow which had just devastated Poland, and urges the deceptiveness of the apparent stagnation along the Maginot and Siegfried Lines. The only defence against it is technical preparedness. The lack of the Allies is tanks and aircraft in sufficient numbers to strike surprise, incisive blows: just as it was lack of these weapons in 1936 and 1938 which enabled Hitler to gain so much without French intervention. As soon as Germany had accumulated enough tanks and aeroplanes to attack the Maginot Line, she would undoubtedly do so. France could be defended not by concrete fortifications alone, but by mechanized power comparable to the German. Even without a direct attack by Germany, French security could be undermined and destroyed by her failure to help other victims of German aggression, until she might be left stranded, a small isolated peninsula in Europe. He ended this summary of what by now were his familiar arguments, made poignant by recent events, with a last appeal for whole-hearted mechanization, even at

[1]As Mr. Theodore Draper has pointed out (*The Six Weeks' War*, p. 228), all his four major works deal rather more with politics and sociology than with military strategy or tactics. De Gaulle the political-soldier was there before de Gaulle the soldier-politician.

that eleventh hour. "In this present conflict and in all previous wars, passivity means defeat. To enable us to act and not merely to take punishment we must produce a new military instrument. Mechanized forces on the ground, in the air and at sea, would enable us to resist German attacks, to raid her strategic bases and key-points, to expel her from any territories she may have subdued, to effect a blockade, and to plunge our swords into her body from all sides."

His memorandum was supported by General Sikorski, Commander-in-Chief of the Polish Army in France, who could speak from bitter experience. But the ears of the High Command, even now, remained as deaf as they had been a decade before. The memorandum was no doubt carefully filed: it was not heeded, and the last few precious months were wasted. The lethargy and complacency of General Gamelin and the French High Command were unbelievable. If accusations of at worst treason and at best criminal negligence were later brought against them, it is not to be wondered at. The Germans, seeing their adoption of Charles de Gaulle's theories of mechanized warfare triumphantly successful in Poland, inevitably set about applying them still more enthusiastically in preparation for the attack on France. And the father of these ideas warned in vain.

* * * * *

And so, with bitterness but not despair in his heart, this brilliant soldier found himself calling from London for all Frenchmen who felt as he did to rally round him and continue the war. Thinking still in large and imperial terms, like his ally Winston Churchill, he reminded his listeners that "France is not alone. She has a vast Empire behind her. She can form a bloc with the British Empire which commands the sea and continues the struggle. She can, like England, utilize without limit the immense industrial resources of the United States. . . . This war is a world war. . . . Struck down to-day by mechanized force, we can in the future gain victory by superior mechanized force."[1] Whilst General de Gaulle was calling for all who could to escape from France, now made into a prison by the armistices with Germany and Italy, Mr. Churchill was arranging for every facility to be given to those who wanted to come. On 24th June he wrote to General Ismay giving instructions for means of escape to be provided. "A sort of 'underground railway' as in the olden days of slavery should be established and a Scarlet Pimpernel organization set up. I have no doubt there will be a steady flow of determined men, and we need all we can get for the defence of the French colonies. The Admiralty and Air Force must co-operate. General de Gaulle and his Committee would of course be the operative authority."[2]

An exchange of letters between Mr. Churchill and General de Gaulle in August led to agreement on the organization, employment and conditions of service of the French volunteer force which the General now set about building up with British aid.

[1]*Discours et Messages du Général de Gaulle* (1942), Vol. I, p. 1.

[2]Winston S. Churchill, *op. cit.*, Vol. II, pp. 193–4. The Committee of which he spoke had been just created. Soon it was given official recognition.

The agreement was embodied in a Memorandum, which came into force as from 1st July, 1940. It was as follows: and is so important for the position of de Gaulle that it is quoted in full.[1]

I

(1) General de Gaulle is engaged in raising a French force composed of volunteers. This force, which includes naval, land and air units, and scientific and technical personnel, will be organized and employed against the common enemies.

(2) This force will never be required to take up arms against France.

II

(1) This force will, as far as possible, retain the character of a French force in respect of personnel, particularly as regards discipline, language, promotion and duties.

(2) So far as may be necessary for their equipment, this force will have priority of allocation as regards property in, and the use of, material (particularly weapons, aircraft, vehicles, ammunition, machinery and supplies) which have already been brought by French armed forces from any quarter, or which may be so brought in the future by such French forces, into territory under the authority of His Majesty's Government in the United Kingdom or into territory where the British High Command exercises authority. In the case of French forces, the command of which has been delegated by agreement between General de Gaulle and the British High Command, no transfer, exchange or reallocation of equipment, property and material in possession of these forces will be made by order of General de Gaulle without prior consultation and agreement with the British High Command.

(3) His Majesty's Government will, as soon as practicable, supply the French force with the additional

[1]Cf. Vice-Admiral Muselier, *De Gaulle contre le Gaullisme* (1946), Annexe VIII, for the texts of the letters and of this Memorandum of 7th August.

equipment which may be essential to equip its units on a scale equivalent to that of British units of the same type.

(4) Naval vessels from the French Fleet will be allocated as follows:—

(*a*) The French force will commission and operate as many vessels as it is able to man.
(*b*) The allocation of the vessels to be commissioned and operated by the French force under (*a*) will be a matter for agreement from time to time between General de Gaulle and the British Admiralty.
(*c*) Vessels not allocated under (*b*) to the French force will be available for commissioning and operating under the direction of the British Admiralty.
(*d*) Of the vessels mentioned under (*c*), some may be operated under direct British control and some may be operated by other Allied naval forces.
(*e*) Vessels operated under British control will, when possible, include in their complement a proportion of French officers and men.
(*f*) All vessels concerned will remain French property.

(5) The possible use of French merchant ships and of their crews, in so far as this is for the purpose of military operations by General de Gaulle's force, will be the subject of arrangements between General de Gaulle and the British departments concerned. Regular contact will be maintained between the Ministry of Shipping and General de Gaulle as regards the use of the rest of the ships and the employment of the merchant seamen.

(6) General de Gaulle, who is in supreme command of the French force, hereby declares that he accepts the general direction of the British High Command. When necessary, he will delegate, in agreement with the British High Command, the immediate command of any part of his force to one or more British officers of appropriate rank, subject to what is stated at the end of Article 1 above.

III

The status of French volunteers will be established in the following manner—

(1) Volunteers will enrol for the duration of the war for the purpose of fighting against the common enemies.

(2) They will receive pay on a basis to be settled separately by agreement between General de Gaulle and the Departments concerned. The period of time during which such rates will apply will be a matter for settlement between General de Gaulle and His Majesty's Government in the United Kingdom.

(3) The volunteers and their dependants will be granted pensions and other benefits in respect of the disablement or death of the volunteers on a basis to be settled by separate agreement between General de Gaulle and the Departments concerned.

(4) General de Gaulle will be entitled to form a civil establishment containing the administrative services required for the organization of his force, the numbers and emoluments of the members of this establishment being settled in consultation with the British Treasury.

(5) The General will also be entitled to recruit technical and scientific staff for war work. The numbers, manner of remuneration and method of employment of this staff will be settled in consultation with the Departments of His Majesty's Government concerned.

(6) His Majesty's Government in the United Kingdom will use their best endeavours at the time of the conclusion of peace, to help the French volunteers to regain any rights, including national status, of which they may have been deprived as a result of their participation in the struggle against the common enemies. His Majesty's Government are willing to afford special facilities to such volunteers to acquire British nationality, and will seek any necessary powers.

IV

(1) Any expenditure incurred for the purpose of the constitution and maintenance of the French force under the provisions of this agreement will be met, in the first instance, by the appropriate Departments of His Majesty's Government in the United Kingdom, which will be entitled to exercise any necessary examination and audit.

(2) The sums required will be regarded as advances and especially recorded; all questions relating to the ultimate settlement of these advances, including any

credits which may be set off by agreement, will be a matter for subsequent arrangement.

V

This agreement shall be regarded as having come into force on the 1st July, 1940.

This was the charter of the Free French Movement. General Spears was commissioned to establish an organization for liaison with the French Organization, and to serve as a link between it and the various British authorities with which de Gaulle would have to deal. Spears was later replaced by Mr. C. Peake of the British Foreign Office. The first response to de Gaulle's call was in some ways disappointing. He was a dim and distant figure to most of the French people, to whom the name of Pétain still held a certain magic appeal. But from the first there were those Frenchmen in England who had been evacuated from Dunkirk and other ports during the collapse of France. Mr. Churchill gave some figures of them in June, 1940. There were some 13,600 naval personnel at Aintree Camp, 5,530 military personnel at Trentham Park, and another 1,900 at Arrow Park. Mr. Churchill ordered them all to be repatriated to Morocco, except that those who wished to serve under de Gaulle could remain in England. "Care must be taken", he ordered, "that no officer or man is sent back into French jurisdiction against his will."[1] On 28th June de Gaulle broadcast the announcement of his formal recognition by the British Government as *le Chef des Français Libres* and declared that he "took under his authority all Frenchmen who are living on

[1]Winston S. Churchill, *op. cit.*, Vol. II, p. 150.

British territory or who shall come to it."[1] The reaction of the new Vichy Government, no doubt under considerable pressure from the Germans, was to get a military court at Clermont Ferrand to pass sentence of military degradation and death on Charles de Gaulle for desertion in time of war and for acts of treason against the State. Marshal Pétain later pretended that this was a mere "act of discipline", to stem an exodus of French officers abroad, and that the sentence was merely one "of principle", never intended to be carried out.[2] Its immediate effect, by making de Gaulle a martyr, was to spread his fame within France and to attract further recruitment for the Free French Forces. When, in October, 1940, some Breton fishermen and their families arrived in England in their boats, they are reported to have said that they had not heard of the General until they were told on the German radio that Vichy had condemned him to death. "Then we said to ourselves, 'That's the man we're looking for. If the Germans insult him he must be all right.' So we secretly crossed the Channel to join him."[3]

Despite the experiences which de Gaulle and Churchill had shared—it had been their common fate to give the alarm about German rearmaments, to urge the creation of adequate mechanized forces, and to be summoned at the last moment to deal with the desperate situation which resulted from neglect of their warnings—they were not by temperament likely to find their intimate association easy or without

[1]*Les Discours et Messages*, Vol. I, p. 7.

[2]Philippe Pétain, *Quatre Années au Pouvoir*, p. 21.

[3]Quoted in Félix de Grand'Combe, *The Three Years of Fighting France* (1943), p. 14.

occasional irritations. Before long there were to be, unfortunately, several tragic occasions for strained relations between the British and their French allies; and these did not make for easy relationships. The posture of the "poor client", in which de Gaulle inevitably found himself, was no easy role for such a man to play. It made him at times exaggeratedly self-assertive, and always nervously prickly. But Mr. Churchill showed insight and understanding. As he later wrote, de Gaulle felt it essential to his position before the French people that he "should maintain a proud and haughty demeanour towards 'perfidious Albion', although an exile, dependent upon our protection and dwelling in our midst. He had to be rude to the British to prove to French eyes that he was not a British puppet. He certainly carried out this policy with perseverance. He even one day explained this technique to me, and I fully comprehended the extraordinary difficulties of his problem. I always admired his massive strength."[1]

There was, too, the problem of his entourage and his followers. Exiles, even those who have courageously sought voluntary exile in order to continue the battle for their own country's honour and liberation, have usually acquired a mentality which, though completely understandable and humanly forgivable, calls for constant patience and imaginative sympathy on the part of their hosts. The Frenchmen who rallied to Carlton Gardens were often quarrelsome, difficult, over-anxious, too ready to see a slight where mere preoccupation with other matters was the real

[1]Winston S. Churchill, *op. cit.*, Vol. II, p. 451. This "technique" has an interesting parallel in Laval's use of British hostility as an alibi in his dealings with the Germans: cf. above, p. 101.

explanation. To act as the focus of such an assemblage of uprooted people in a foreign country was a task which would have made heavy drafts upon the tact of a man more tactful by nature than is Charles de Gaulle. He earned a reputation, since transferred to Russian Foreign Ministers, for saying "No" too firmly and too often. Yet the whole significance of the man and his position was that he had uttered a resounding "No" to Hitler, Vichy, and defeat: and it would have been unreasonable to expect such qualities not to bring with them their corresponding impediments.

This was what Mr. Churchill understood, and characteristically was so ready to forgive: but there were to be many moments, especially in 1943, when the patience both of Churchill and of Roosevelt was very sorely tried by the absurdly aggressive and inept methods of de Gaulle and his followers. The Gaullist press, especially *La Marseillaise* published in London, was apt to sustain most untimely attacks on Britain and still more on the United States. It was always excitable and often irresponsible. In the spring of 1943 it was eventually banned and had to be transplanted to Algiers, where it started its ill-favoured work all over again. In May, Churchill, in his speech to Congress, praised Giraud but significantly omitted to mention de Gaulle. In July, 1943, the Washington *Post* published an article announcing that Churchill had drafted a document which would prepare public opinion in the Allied countries for the liquidation of Gaullism, on the grounds that de Gaulle could no longer be considered a reliable friend of Britain, that he had tried to play off Britain and the United States one against the other, and that he had "Fascist and dictatorial tendencies". Questioned about this in the House of Commons on 21st July, Mr. Churchill said, "I assume full responsibility for this document. I myself drew up the text. It is a confidential document. I am not ready to discuss it other than in secret meeting, and only if such is the general desire of the House." No official text of this interesting document has yet been published, but its existence and its general purport are certain enough.

By reason both of his inherent position, his personal temperament, and the character of his entourage and his adherents, General de Gaulle's relations with his allies therefore suffered a series of tensions and crises. The story of his achievements between 1940 and 1945 is a great one. He succeeded in establishing, outside the prison-camp that France became, a focus of hope and of loyalty for the thousands of brave resisters scattered throughout France. He created a *mystique* of "Gaullism" which was to have a profound effect upon his own character and upon the fate of post-war France. If he sometimes overstrained this loyalty, as when he called for not very timely and not very successful "lightning strikes" or demonstrations, yet his central achievement remains unchallenged: his was the name that brave men uttered as a symbol of their resolve to reject defeat. Ingenious young Frenchmen found new ways of tormenting their German oppressors that included such pathetic gestures of defiance as carrying two poles (*deux gaulles*) in processions. His too was the voice which they risked tortures to listen to on their secret wireless sets. The Gaullist *mystique* was, indeed, largely the creation of radio: a peculiarly modern phenomenon.

on the worst possible terms with these Allies without whom the liberation of France—the one objective for which Gaullism was founded—would most certainly have been impossible. It is a striking record of apparent ineptitude, calling for more serious examination and explanation than any writer other than Kerillis has so far attempted. It is the task of this study to examine these vicissitudes not in an effort to extol or condemn de Gaulle, but in an attempt to assess his significance and to reach an interpretation of how these events influenced his character and his ambitions.

* * * * *

The qualities of a leader may to some extent be judged by his relations with his highest colleagues. While the withdrawal from Dunkirk and the making of the armistice with Germany were still so recent, French attention naturally concentrated on the Navy—their vital link with the overseas territories of France. Vice-Admiral Muselier, who escaped from France on 23rd June to Gibraltar, and thence to London, was commissioned by de Gaulle to take charge of the Free French naval forces. He has given a somewhat biting picture of his first impressions of de Gaulle. "I was immediately struck by the physique of the man: by his great height, with a disproportionately small head and a too low forehead; his eyes, small and grey, do not frankly return one's gaze and always turn away before replying to precise questions. His chin, of very unusual shape, does not indicate strong will; his enunciation is slow, as if he were listening to himself speaking; and his mouth, medium in size, sometimes opens quite round to show irregular teeth. His nose is powerful, almost Bourbon. His ears, badly shaped, stick out widely."[1] But he adds that the General's amiable reception and evident resolve to carry on the war against Germany won him over at once. Muselier found that he could muster, in all, a hundred naval craft of all types and tonnage, and some 15,000 men. It was a not inconsiderable force, at a moment when every instrument of war was valuable. He records, however, that many more of the governors and administrators of the colonial territories might have been won over to resistance, but for certain blunders and but for "the ambition of General de Gaulle to be the absolute master of the France of tomorrow".[2]

The gist of Admiral Muselier's basic charge against de Gaulle is the same as the charge of Kerillis: according to the agreement of 7th August all who rallied to the Free French Forces regarded themselves as joining a purely military organization; according to the terms of this agreement, they were promised they would never be called upon to take up arms against other Frenchmen; but General de Gaulle, "having marched his troops against French troops on several occasions, and having transformed his movement into a political movement, the verbal agreements, written or otherwise, legally became null and void".[3] It was de Gaulle's anxiety to secure a territorial basis for his movement on overseas French soil, and to prevent the French Empire from falling under enemy influence or control, which embroiled him in

[1]Vice-Admiral Muselier, *op. cit.*, p. 13. Cf. the very similar description in Maurice Martin du Gard, *La Carte Imperiale*, pp. 165–6.

[2]*Ibid.*, p. 17.

[3]Vice-Admiral Muselier, *op. cit.*, p. 71.

this dilemma. The climax was the fiasco of his attack on Dakar, the key port of French West Africa.

The background to this important adventure is still somewhat obscure: but certain facts are clear enough. Perhaps the basic fact is that the tragedy of Mers-el-Kébir, in July, had made some combined Franco-British action diplomatically desirable, and yet it had at the same time hardened the attitude of the colonial administrators towards Britain and the Free French.[1] The British Government, as Mr. Churchill has recorded, attached great importance to aiding the Free French to rally overseas territories, and de Gaulle was more than eager to prove his forces in action. It was believed, on the best available information and advice, that if the Free French flag were raised in West Africa and if Dakar were occupied, the influential forces of French West Africa would swing over to the Allies. Mr. Churchill as early as the beginning of August, 1940, gave general approval for such a plan. It was at first planned that all the troops involved should be French, numbering some 2,500 men; but in the event this force had to be backed by British troops. Churchill has accepted a major share of responsibility for the plan, remarking, "I thus undertook in an exceptional degree the initiation and advocacy of the Dakar expedition, to which the code name 'Menace' was assigned. Of this, although I cannot feel we were well served on all occasions and certainly had bad luck, I never at any

[1]The effects of the British action at Oran and Mers-el-Kébir, when powerful units of the French Fleet were destroyed and many French lives unfortunately lost, were great both at Vichy and among the Free French. See Winston S. Churchill, *op. cit.*, Vol. II, pp. 208–11; Maurice Martin du Gard, *op. cit.*, pp. 33–41; A. Kammerer, *La Tragédie de Mers-el-Kébir* (1943).

time repented. Dakar was a prize, rallying the French colonial empire a greater. There was a fair chance of gaining these results without bloodshed, and I felt in my finger-tips that Vichy France would not declare war. . . . The most serious danger was prolonged fighting."[1] Muselier, charged with the naval planning of an operation in which he had not been consulted, insisted that it was possible only if it could be carried out without bloodshed: so that favourable political conditions must precede the military operation.[2] Here, indeed, was an especially acute example of the inter-twining of military and political forces, involving for success a nice computation of the balance between the two. The scheme was, moreover, one which might in the event lead to Frenchmen fighting Frenchmen. But as little daunted by the prospect of such dangers as Churchill himself, de Gaulle went ahead with his plan. The arrival of the Anglo-French armada at Dakar was fixed for dawn on 19th September, 1940.

From the outset things went wrong. There were unexpected delays in starting. There were leakages of information, partly through the Free French troops. Above all, by a curious succession of mistakes and accidents, three French cruisers and three destroyers from Toulon passed unmolested and at full speed through the straits of Gibraltar and reached harbour at Dakar on 14th September before they could be intercepted by any of the available British naval forces. Mr. Churchill's immediate impulse was to abandon the whole enterprise in view of this changed situation. "The whole scheme of a bloodless

[1]Winston S. Churchill, *op. cit.*, Vol. II, p. 422.
[2]Vice-Admiral Muselier, *op. cit.*, p. 77.

landing and occupation by General de Gaulle seemed to me ruined by the arrival of the French squadron, probably carrying reinforcements, good gunners, and bitter-minded Vichy officers, to decide the Governor, to pervert the garrison, and man the batteries."[1] But all the commanders on the spot, General de Gaulle most vehemently of all, protested against abandoning the plan. Major-General Irwin reported that de Gaulle "has also committed himself to complete co-operation with British troops in case of need, and he has not shirked responsibility for fighting between Frenchmen". The War Cabinet agreed to let the commanders on the spot carry out their wishes. On 23rd September, in a fog, the approach to Dakar began. British planes dropped tricolour leaflets on the port, which appear, by accounts of the reactions to them, to have been ill-conceived as propaganda.[2] Seven of de Gaulle's emissaries landed on the local airfield, and were immediately arrested by the forewarned Vichy troops. One of them had in his possession a list of the leading Gaullist supporters, most of whom were also promptly rounded up. The Governor-General, Pierre Boisson, proclaimed a state of siege. The Anglo-French naval force approached through the fog to within five thousand yards. A shore battery opened fire on it, and the fire was returned. Exchange of fire continued for about an hour-and-a-half, then the naval force withdrew. Later in the day de Gaulle tried to land troops at Rufisque, but failed. The attack on the port of Dakar, and on the French ships there which included the battleship *Richelieu*, was

[1]Winston S. Churchill, *op. cit.*, Vol. II, p. 427.
[2]Cf. Vice-Admiral Muselier, *op. cit.*, pp. 84, 88.

resumed the next day, and the next again. *Barham* and *Resolution* were both damaged, and in return the *Richelieu* had been hit, a light cruiser set on fire, two submarines sunk, two destroyers burnt, and the port bombarded. On 25th it was decided to call off the whole engagement.

The whole incident was the result of an accumulation of misjudgments and misfortunes, and it would be useless to try to allocate responsibility for the fiasco. It enabled Vichy to claim considerable credit with the Germans for its vigour in defending the colonial empire against allied forces, and convinced Hitler that Vichy's fight with de Gaulle was genuine.[1] It did much to discredit de Gaulle with British opinion, although as Mr. Churchill's subsequent account shows it would be unjust to hold him mainly responsible: and as Churchill said in the House of Commons at the time, de Gaulle's conduct and bearing had increased his confidence in the leader of the Free French. A fortnight later de Gaulle established himself in the Cameroons, and made it a rallying point for the Free French. As French Equatorial Africa had already been led into the Free French camp by its remarkable negro Governor, Eboué, the movement now had a large area of French overseas territory under its control, and had become a responsible administrative authority instead of merely a volunteer fighting movement. The whole Dakar incident, as Churchill suggests, "illustrates in a high degree . . .

[1]*Ciano's Diplomatic Papers*, p. 400: "At one time he (i.e., Hitler) had asked himself the question whether the fight between the Vichy Government and General de Gaulle were genuine or a sham. From various sources, and particularly from the evidence of films of the battles of Oran and Dakar, he has reached the conclusion that the fight is genuine."

the interplay of military and political forces". That made it an explosive mixture, and had de Gaulle drawn the correct lessons from his experience of handling so explosive a mixture he might have evaded further predicaments in which he was soon to find himself.

The next area in which a similar situation was to arise was an area of which he himself had direct experience—the Levant. Syria and the Lebanon were in a special position for two reasons. They were not part of "France overseas", but were held by France under mandate; and they were a part of the world in which French suspicions of British designs on their interests were particularly acute. The Vichy French High Commissioner there was General Dentz. In September, 1940, General Catroux was appointed Free French High Commissioner for the Middle East. In a press-conference in June, 1945, de Gaulle claimed to have been directly responsible for the intervention: "it is Free France which took the initiative to enter Syria in 1941, leading England in her train." But on 22nd September, 1940, Churchill sent this telegram to de Gaulle, who was then about to attack Dakar.

> From every quarter the presence of General Catroux was demanded in Syria. I therefore took the responsibility in your name of inviting the General to go there. It is of course perfectly understood that he holds his position only from you, and I shall make this clear to him again. Sometimes one has to take decisions on the spot because of their urgency and the difficulty of explaining to others at a distance. There is time to stop him still if you desire it, but I should consider this was a very unreasonable act.[1]

As with Dakar, it was above all anxiety lest a key strategic point should, through Vichy auspices, fall

[1]Winston S. Churchill, *op. cit.*, Vol. II, Appendix A, p. 596.

under German or Italian control, which in the first instance prompted British action.

In August an Italian armistice commission had arrived in Beirut. Axis influence greatly increased, and the British blockade was extended to Syria and Lebanon. The area became a focus of tension by the end of 1940. After Vichy France withdrew from the League of Nations in April, 1941, it could be argued that the juridical basis of the mandatory power had disappeared. By that time internal unrest, due to a combination of nationalist agitation and economic distress, forced General Dentz to overhaul the governmental system and to issue a statement that he recognized eventual independence as the aim of French rule in Syria. Soon after a corresponding change took place in Lebanon. The next month German aircraft were permitted to use Syrian air-bases as stages on their journey to Iraq, in support of the revolt of Raschid Ali. In June, therefore, a mixed force of British Empire and Free French troops, under General Sir Henry Maitland Wilson and General Catroux, crossed the frontiers. The Vichy forces under General Dentz put up unexpectedly strong resistance, and again it happened that Free French predictions about the bad morale and ready surrender of Vichy troops were proved over-optimistic. Within a month, however, Dentz was forced to seek an armistice, which was signed at Acre on 14th July, 1941. It enabled allied forces to occupy Syria and Lebanon. The military operations came to an end: but the political complications had just begun.[1]

[1]For an excellent examination of the whole problem, see A. H. Hourani, *Syria and Lebanon: A Political Essay* (1946).

When entering the territory General Catroux issued a proclamation in the course of which he declared: "I come to put an end to the mandatory regime and to proclaim you free and independent. You will therefore be from henceforward sovereign and independent peoples, and you will be able either to form yourselves into independent States or to unite into a single State. In either event, your independent and sovereign status will be guaranteed by a Treaty in which our mutual relations will be defined. This Treaty will be negotiated as soon as possible between your representatives and myself." At the same time the British Ambassador in Cairo announced: "I am authorized by His Majesty's Government to declare that they support and associate themselves with the assurance of independence given by General Catroux on behalf of General de Gaulle to Syria and Lebanon." The formal independence of Syria was duly proclaimed in September, and of Lebanon in November, 1941. Neither elicited much enthusiasm from the population, for in war-time conditions substantial French military control continued, and the nationalists preferred to wait sceptically and see how far material concessions of self-government would be carried out. Constitutional life was not restored, nor was power transferred to the new Syrian and Lebanese Governments, until August and September, 1943. By November the representatives of General de Gaulle were engaged in arresting the Lebanese President and most of his ministers, suspending the new constitution, and dealing with a general strike which broke out as a result of this drastic action.

Most of the Lebanese Deputies retired to a

mountain stronghold and organized an armed nationalist force. General Catroux had to intervene, and the President and Ministers were reinstated. By the beginning of 1944 both States had been granted real powers of self-government, and by the end of that year a series of special agreements had completed the transition, except for the thorny problem of control over the *troupes spéciales*, the best organized native military forces in the territory. In the end the political and constitutional problems were fairly satisfactorily settled; but only in the end.[1] Meantime the issuing of general statements of principle followed by disappointing concessions of substance had cast doubts upon the reliability of the Free French, and even suspicions upon their sincerity. Imprisonment of the new President and Government seemed a strange way to inaugurate independence and sovereignty. Even allowing for the consequences of sheer confusion, which gave a false impression of insincerity, the incidents still further lowered the prestige of de Gaulle. Worse than that, it made all his allies and potential allies take precautions against similar behaviour in future, in their dealings with him.

The fruit of this reaction is seen in two further incidents which may be taken as representative of the whole tendency. One is the British action in Madagascar in 1942; the other is what happened in Indo-China. Mr. Churchill is reported to have justified the British attack on Diego, in Madagascar, without Free French aid, by saying to de Gaulle, "We hoped that resistance would be less if we presented ourselves alone and we had to conform to the views of

[1]See below, p. 209.

America."[1] Having captured Diego, Churchill wanted to go no further, but de Gaulle opposed any idea of a compromise with the Vichy administrators of the island, led by the Governor-General Annet. When an armistice had been signed, de Gaulle was allowed to appoint General Legentilhomme as the Free French High Commissioner for Madagascar. The whole British initiative betokened uneasy relations with de Gaulle and proclaimed this to the world.

In Indo-China Admiral Decoux had been, in July, 1940, appointed Governor-General by Darlan, in place of General Catroux. As he has described in his very remarkable book, *À la barre de l'Indochine*, he contrived to preserve the integrity and independence of his rule by persistent obstruction of any attempts by Japanese, Siamese, and Chinese to assert control over the territory. He took the view, so instinctive and so general amongst French overseas administrators and service-chiefs, that his duty was to continue allegiance to the government which ruled metropolitan France, whilst preserving his territory intact to hand over eventually to the legitimate government of post-war France. He refused to accord any allegiance to the Free French movement, which he regarded as an illegitimate and upstart authority. He kept on good terms with the native rulers of Indo-China, and was given the honorific title of "Prince-Protector of the Empire" of Annam. In August, 1944, he took part in drawing up a statement which was sent secretly to de Gaulle to inform him of the situation in Indo-China. It emphasized the need, in French

[1]Cf. J. Soustelle, *De Londres à Alger* (1944), p. 339; and M. Martin du Gard, *op. cit.*, pp. 239–74.

interests, to preserve order and peace there, and to avoid any drastic changes of authority.[1] He has given a bitter account of his interview with de Gaulle in October, 1945, a week after his arrival in France.[2] General de Gaulle was by then Head of the Provisional Government of France. His reception was frigid, and without even a handshake. After a long monologue, in which Decoux described his role in Indo-China from 1940 until 1945, de Gaulle admitted that he had fully resisted the Japanese, but added, "You have, however, committed several mistakes, which I shall indicate to you." One was to have remained at his post as Governor-General after the armistice of 1940: the only patriots are those who came to London to serve de Gaulle. Another was to have stayed on at his post in 1941, when it became apparent that Marshal Pétain could do nothing against Germany or Japan: "but as you did not come to me, I had to appeal to others." The third was that he had unnecessarily praised Pétain and consistently echoed *Vive le Maréchal!*

In vain did Decoux try to explain that to have abandoned his post would have handed over Indo-China and the French interests there to Japanese control; that to have openly joined the Free French movement before it was in a position to defend Indo-China from disorder or from foreign attack would have been no service to France; and that the symbol of Pétain had enabled him to preserve allegiance to France amongst the 25 million Indo-Chinese to whom the name of de Gaulle would have meant nothing.

[1]For full text, see Admiral Decoux, *À la barre de l'Indochine*, p. 497.
[2]*Ibid.*, pp. 476–81.

He might have added that the ill-success of de Gaulle at Dakar and in Syria had been noted. There was no room for such ideas left in the mind of de Gaulle by 1945. He still viewed the whole conflict in terms of black and white, of moral absolutes. Everyone who had not been openly for him had been against him: and everyone who had followed a form of resistance different from his own absolute and defiant hostility to Vichy was suspect of treason. It is impossible to acquit the General of the charge of extreme arrogance of mind and *naïveté* of political judgment. The situation in France after 1940, and still more in the overseas territories, was so complex, so shrouded in uncertainties, so tinged with half-lights, that political absolutes had little place in them. Resistance to Germany and Japan could take many forms, and it was all the more effective for being so variegated. To have forced the issues and clarified the position too soon would in many cases have ill-served British or French interests. Yet this is precisely what de Gaulle kept insisting ought to be done.

By importing into French affairs after June, 1940, this absolutist outlook and this refusal to compromise over the mode of resistance which might be most appropriate and effective in each part of France's scattered overseas territories, he ignored the realities of the situation, both psychological and military. The attitude that Laval adopted was, naturally, utterly incomprehensible to him: for it was at the opposite pole of political method. To insist in soldierly way on settling such issues by force at a time when the preponderance of power was still in favour of Vichy or of the enemy was the certain way to court disaster.

The agents and emissaries whom he sent into the colonial territories to stir up and organize local resistance served only to challenge the forces of law and order there, and led to local fighting between Frenchmen. It alienated the sympathies of colonial administrations which, left to themselves, had no affection or favour for the enemy. It discredited French prestige with the colonial peoples, and thereby stored up difficulties for himself and his successors after liberation. It was a dubious policy somewhat recklessly pursued, however worthy may have been its moral intentions. It led him into a position where he had no defence against the charge levied by Muselier and Kerillis that he had betrayed his original undertaking, contained in the very foundation-charter of the Free French, that the volunteer force would not be used to fight Frenchmen.

It is this propensity to indulge in premature and ill-considered meddling in overseas resistance which is the most common complaint of the colonial administrations. Admiral Decoux writes: "The abandonment of their posts by French officers, provoked by Gaullist propaganda, became increasingly frequent in 1942–1943 along the Chinese-Tonkin frontier, creating a dangerous psychosis of desertion." This, at a time of dangerous tension between China and Indo-China, did nothing to win over the Government-General to the Gaullist cause. After the liberation of France the appointment of new French officials in Indo-China was carried out clumsily. Decoux hoped that there might be reconciliation between Pétain and de Gaulle, which would have healed the divisions in so many colonial territories. But in November, 1944, he was sent ambiguous and oddly involved instructions from the new Provisional Government of France to whom he had proclaimed his loyalty. He was secretly ordered not to resign his post, but to ignore meantime the existence of the Gaullist emissaries and secret agents, General Mordant and General Aymé, from whom he would nevertheless receive orders later.[1] It made his personal position and his official performance of duties virtually impossible. Behind these strange arrangements, as behind so many of the Gaullist mistakes in the colonies, lay a fundamental ignorance of conditions on the spot, no less than a misunderstanding of the administrators' psychology. It was, in the inflamed nationalisms of the middle east and of Asia, playing with fire; fire which was later to burn his own fingers.

Equally unfortunate was the policy of Gaullism, manifest both in the treatment of the crew of the *Richelieu* when it sailed to New York for repairs and in the treatment of the North African Army of Giraud in 1943, to encourage French sailors and soldiers to desert from their existing units. In both cases, this policy was pursued after these units had been formally brought into the war on the Allied side. The naval consequences were to immobilize and endanger the French ships concerned, to such an extent that in March the United States Secretary of the Navy, Mr. Frank Knox, had to protest publicly against the Gaullist encouragement of desertions. In July the General Staff of the African Army prepared a report on the methods and results of Gaullist efforts to seduce soldiers away from the Giraudist Army. It described the methods—promises of bonuses, offers of

[1]Full text in Decoux, *op. cit.*, p. 309.

promotion, increased pay—by which soldiers were induced to desert to the Free French Forces. And according to this report in Algeria alone some 2,750 men had been thus seduced. It became clear that de Gaulle could suffer no authority which was a potential rival to himself; and that to destroy any such authority he was prepared to sacrifice national unity and military efficiency to a jealous regard for selfish and partisan interests. It was a paradoxical and fatal policy for a movement which had originated in pure patriotism.

One final and picturesquely piratical exploit calls for some examination: the excursion of Admiral Muselier to the islands of Saint-Pierre and Miquelon off the Newfoundland coast. Quarrels between de Gaulle and his chief naval commander, Muselier, became only too frequent by the end of 1941. Muselier accused him of aiming at excessive personal power, and de Gaulle clearly distrusted the Admiral's own personal ambitions. Their disputes reached a crisis in September, 1941, when they disagreed violently about the composition of the new Committee of National Liberation. It was the climax of a long series of trivial and tedious personal differences about petty details of promotions, decorations and titles. Muselier threatened to link up his naval forces with the British and leave the new Gaullist Committee. This evoked a haughty and threatening reply. Through the mediation of British naval authorities the quarrel was patched up: but de Gaulle was left only too ready to seize any opportunity to get rid of the awkward admiral. The attack on Saint-Pierre and Miquelon had the double merit of taking Muselier far away from London, and perhaps of embroiling him in difficulties with the Americans and the British. In so far as there was any such intention on de Gaulle's part, it was unwise, for the embarrassment recoiled upon himself in the end.[1]

In November, 1941, Muselier set off for Canada and the United States, with the aim of getting their governments to agree to his plans. The Americans regarded the plans as inopportune and said so, but the Canadians seemed more favourable. M. de Bournat, the Governor of the islands, and Admiral Robert, the Vichy officer responsible for the security of the Antilles and other western islands, were typical of their class, and regarded it as their duty to preserve allegiance to the government of metropolitan France. The British, like the Americans, saw little to be gained, and perhaps trouble to be caused, by disturbing these two tiny islands which were not threatened in any way by the enemy, and were within easy protective range of North America. But in December de Gaulle telegraphed to Muselier, "I order you to proceed to rally Saint-Pierre and Miquelon by means at your own disposal and without consulting foreigners. I take the entire responsibility for this operation which has become indispensable to the preservation for France of her possessions."[2] Muselier replied, "Your orders will be carried out as rapidly as possible; but I am held up by a violent snow-storm." At dawn on Christmas Eve, in the midst of the bleak North-Atlantic winter which these little islands suffer, there sailed into the harbour four warships flying the Cross

[1]For accounts of the business, see Vice-Admiral Muselier, *op. cit.*, pp. 246–316; M. Martin du Gard, *op. cit.*, pp. 223–37.

[2]M. Martin du Gard, *op. cit.*, p. 229.

of Lorraine. The islands were virtually undefended, and the three-hundred-and-fifty invaders had no difficulty in taking over the islands. A farcical plebiscite was held on Boxing Day, wherein the simple fishermen were asked to vote for either *France Libre* or *Puissances de l'Axe.* Over a third abstained from voting, some crossed out the word *Libre* and voted simply for France, others wrote *Vive Pétain et de Gaulle*, but these last two choices were disqualified. Eleven voted for the "Axis Powers". The Department of State and the American press received the news with a mixture of anger and amusement. The clergy of the islands put up passive resistance, as did the most eminent men of the islands. Under pressure from the United States and Great Britain, Muselier was recalled, and before long was engaged in an open quarrel with General de Gaulle. The islands were taken under the joint supervision of Canada and the United States for the rest of the war. It was a comic anti-climax to the brave exploits of the Free French Admiral, and to the excessively self-assertive antics of both. But it was the breach of a specific promise given to his allies by de Gaulle.[1]

The story of the relations between Admiral Muselier and General de Gaulle, which the Admiral has told in all its sordidly petty detail,[2] casts little credit on either of them, but least of all on de Gaulle's immediate entourage. To have got embroiled at all in so bitterly personal a squabble with one of his leading and most sincere and able supporters was severe condemnation of the General's capacities for political leadership. But worse than that, the story reveals

[1]W. S. Churchill, *op. cit.*, Vol. III, p. 666; W. L. Langer, *op. cit.*, pp. 212-21.
[2]Vice-Admiral Muselier, *op. cit.*, pp. 359–387.

something of the sinister and intriguing personalities who had collected around the enigmatic but autocratic personality of General de Gaulle. Even when everything possible has been allowed for the inevitable anxiety neuroses and traditional extremism of *emigrés*, and for the fine work done by some of the patriots amongst the Free French, there remains a squalid residue of jostling, power-loving people who brought nothing but harm and ill-fame to the movement and to the reputation of its leader. The nature of some of these insidious influences appeared in the sensational arrest of Admiral Muselier himself, in January, 1941, by British officials of Scotland Yard. He was arrested on allegations of treachery and espionage brought by certain members of de Gaulle's entourage. The evidence produced was documents purporting to come from General Rozoy, an agent of Vichy, but actually they were forged; and it was the result—according to the Admiral[1]—of a plot hatched at Carlton Gardens by a number of individuals in the security-service of de Gaulle. The Admiral spent eight days in prison or under guard, and was released with a letter of apologies and regrets from Mr. Eden. His release was soon followed by an invitation to dine with Mr. Churchill, and he was received in audience by the King. Nor was he the only victim of the machinations at Carlton Gardens.[2] The vacillations and weak tolerance of General de Gaulle in face of these scandalous intrigues reflected credit neither on his intelligence nor on his capacity for political leadership.

There grew up at Carlton Gardens a "court", with

[1]Vice-Admiral Muselier, *op. cit.*, pp. 138–57, where relevant documents are also printed.

[2]H. de Kerillis, *I accuse de Gaulle*, pp. 25–31, for mention of these other incidents.

many of the same courtly characteristics which were to be found in the entourage of Marshal Pétain at Vichy. Courtiers are prone to much the same vices whoever may form the hub of a court, and it was a situation which was hardened and made all the more dangerous when the court moved, after November, 1942, to Algiers. There it had important territories to govern, and the intrigues and machinations had a peculiarly fertile soil because of the juxtaposition of Vichy or ex-Vichy officials and politicians with the Free French, and because of the opportunist policy followed by the United States authorities from the very beginning of their occupation of North Africa. President Roosevelt's "temporary expedient" of the deal with Admiral Darlan in November, followed by the irruption of General Giraud into the subtle politics of the Provisional French Committee, created a tangle of jostling forces and personalities. They produced immense gossip and countless sensational "scandals". The atmosphere has been remarkably well described and illustrated by the French journalist, Renée Pierre-Gosset, in her book *Algiers, 1941–1943: A Temporary Expedient.* During the period of General Weygand's rule in North Africa, and that of Yves Chatel which followed Weygand's recall in November, 1941, Algeria had become the happy hunting-ground for every sort of wild intrigue. "The atmosphere was quite unreal and utterly unbelievable to people who did not live through it. Enemies rubbed shoulders with each other, hundreds of plots were laid, the police were taking violent measures of repression in a musical comedy setting."[1] It was a crazy "neutral"

[1]Renée Pierre-Gosset, *op. cit.*, p. 22.

enclave in a crazy world, with a tremendous black market and every sort of corruption, espionage and counter-espionage in the purest Hollywood traditions. Mingled with it was the revolting cruelty practised by the most out-and-out Vichy supporters, in police and civil administration, upon luckless resisters who fell into their hands. The prisons and labour-camps of the Trans-Saharan Railway were death-traps to many of the noblest young patriots who were trying to escape to join General de Gaulle. Here too there was recurrent bloodshed between Frenchmen, and it left a legacy of bitterness which much affected the transplanted court of de Gaulle.

It was sound prudence which restricted the first troops of invasion to the Americans and British, and which kept General de Gaulle even in ignorance of the whole scheme until it had been carried out. One who had from the first resisted in North Africa declared, "If a landing had been attempted by the Gaullists, it would have meant the outbreak of a dreadful civil war."[1] The incident of Dakar was not forgotten in England, nor that of Saint-Pierre and Miquelon forgiven in the United States. Yet the exclusion of de Gaulle from an active share in this major operation had, in turn, certain unfortunate results. The "deal" between General Mark Clark and the double-dealing Darlan was a sordid and dubious arrangement, bringing certain temporary and limited material advantages but a positive loss of moral integrity to the allied cause. It has been customary to lay all responsibility (and censure) for the decision on the Americans, and it was indeed they who had

[1]*Ibid.*, p. 39; cf. W. L. Langer, *op. cit.*, pp. 290ff.

to take this burdensome decision. It remains to be seen whether the historian, from his vantage point of subsequent retrospection, may not see in the previous ill-advised behaviour of General de Gaulle some share of responsibility for such a course being chosen by the Americans.

Whoever may bear the main burden of responsibility, the consequences of the Darlan deal were clear enough at once. The easy occupation of North Africa was a great military advantage: but it did not prevent fighting, and it caused widespread moral bewilderment. As Professor Denis Brogan wrote at that time: "The news that MM. Flandin, Pucheu, Peyrouton and, possibly, other late leading lights in Vichy have had a sudden Damascus conversion has added to the bewilderment of the innocent spectator. . . . It will take a good deal to persuade me that a future France, holding up her head among the nations, has more need of the timid, the prudent, the despairing men of Vichy than it has of the men who adopted for themselves and for their country, not the imbecile craftiness of '*la France seule*' of Maurras, but '*honneur et patrie*.' "[1] General de Gaulle, in a broadcast from his own station at Brazzaville, pointed the moral which he drew. "The nation will not tolerate that a handful of men who symbolize capitulation, collaboration and usurpation, who have used and abused the discipline of others in order to fight France's liberators, should use and abuse it now to ape honour and duty. The nation will not allow these men, who failed in war against foreign Powers and sense themselves doomed, to safeguard their own future by creating

[1] D. W. Brogan, *French Personalities and Problems* (1946), pp. 156–7.

conditions which would end in civil war. The nation does not recognise their authority, derived from a grotesque parody of divine right through the alleged reincarnation of a Buddha, whom, moreover, they betray and who, into the bargain, condemns them. Hitler said he wanted to 'rot away our war'. The nation does not want anyone to rot away our liberation."[1] De Gaulle had by now become in France the symbol of continuous resistance to Germany, of complete refusal to accept the defeat of 1940 as final. Gaullism had acquired that most potent of qualities in France—a *mystique*. It was important that this symbol should not be smirched by any hint of compromise with the new-found patriotism of Darlan and his colleagues. This time the General's single-mindedness proved of value to him and to his cause and country. He would refuse to make terms with Darlan, even if his allies had: and he was saved from the material disadvantages of this decision by the timely assassination of Darlan by young Bonnier de la Chapelle on Christmas Eve, and by the equally timely arrival in North Africa of General Giraud with whom it was more possible and much more seemly to come to an understanding.[2] Two days after Darlan's death

[1]*Speeches of General de Gaulle*, Vol. II, 6th December, 1942. The last reference is to Darlan's repudiation of Pétain's orders, and Pétain's consequent disavowal of Darlan. It was claimed in the trial of Pétain that, when formally protesting to Mr. Tuck against the United States action in North Africa, he gave Tuck a little tap on the shoulder and slyly hummed a few bars of *La Marseillaise*! (*Le Procès*, p. 253).

[2]It will be remembered that Giraud, though sixty-three, had made a remarkable escape from his German prison at Koenigstein in April, 1942, and had arrived at Vichy, to the great embarrassment of Pétain, at the end of that month. Having made his peace with the Marshal by a somewhat ambiguously worded letter of "submission", he was allowed to live at home in France, until he slipped out by submarine to Gibraltar on 5th November. He was, from the first, an important personality in the whole "expedient". The story of his role in North Africa and of his relations with General de Gaulle is told by G. Ward Price in *Giraud and the African Scene* (1944).

Giraud was elected High Commissioner of France in Africa by the Imperial Council in Algiers. He was to combine these political duties with the military duties of Commander-in-Chief of the North African Troops which he was already performing.

The story of the relations between General de Gaulle and General Giraud is a new phase in the evolution both of the French National Committee and of de Gaulle himself as a political leader. During the perplexing weeks between the emergence of Darlan in North Africa and his assassination, Giraud as military chief kept repeating to journalists, "I am a soldier. I will have nothing to do with politics." De Gaulle, by now, was adopting the view that "there is no war without politics". From his experience of heading the Free French, he had drawn this lesson: Giraud, some six months out of his prison, had not. He began by taking the politically absurd view that, for the time, everybody was to remain in their place: "political prisoners in prison, Gaullists in London, and Vichyites in power", as Renée Pierre-Gosset pungently puts it. He was determined not to lead a revolutionary movement, and wanted to do nothing which might impede or complicate military operations. Gaullism, by now, had acquired all the qualities of a restlessly revolutionary movement, and as this is the essential clue to all that happened afterwards it is important to understand how this remarkable change had come about.

Charles de Gaulle's original act of defiance, in June, 1940, was of course in itself a revolutionary act. But it was some considerable time before the implications of it, as involving logically and inevitably a programme of revolutionary overhaul in France itself, came to be appreciated even by de Gaulle himself. Professor Brogan put the point clearly a few months after the North African landings when he wrote: "Without any planning, the de Gaulle movement became the chief, not the only but the chief, symbol of the under-privileged, the people of France, the people Admiral Leahy and Robert Murphy did not meet. It may not have deserved to be the chief symbol; it is not and never has been the only symbol. Its role was threatened when Hitler invaded Russia. With all European peoples (including the English) the Russian resistance has been the great, heroic theme of this war. But the effect in France was to help the resistance movement, that is, to help de Gaulle. The Germans aided by shooting people indiscriminately as Communists or de Gaullists. Often their victims were neither. But the identification stuck. The Russians were the people who knew the answers concealed from Gamelin, Weygand and Pétain. The de Gaullists were the people who had never spoken well of the Germans, unlike MM. Pétain, Darlan and Laval. . . . Jacobinism, that is, revolutionary patriotism, was forced on the de Gaullist movement, especially after the beginning of the Russian war."[1] In his speech in the Albert Hall to a rally of French people on Armistice Day, 1942, de Gaulle chose to strike the authentic note of revolutionary Jacobinism, showing that he had at least by now appreciated the new role of his movement. "France knows, too, the cost of a regime whose social and moral fibres had hardened, so that the country first suffered from the indifference

[1]D. W. Brogan, *op. cit.*, p. 144, and cf. Jacques Debû-Bridel, *Les Partis contre Charles de Gaulle* (1948), p. 21.

of the exploited masses and was then betrayed by coalitions of trusts and men in power. She means to establish at home a social and moral system in which each individual can live in dignity and security, and where no monopoly can exploit him or in any way obstruct the general interests." He spoke of setting up a "new democracy in which the sovereignty of the people may be fully exercised by election and control".[1]

The prolonged contest between de Gaulle and Giraud for leadership of the French National Committee accentuated this transformation of what had been initially a pure resistance organization into a political movement. Compared with the non-political Giraud, de Gaulle emerged as an astute politician. His movement gradually transformed itself from a non-party into something of an all-party movement. Springing originally from his personal enterprise, it had grown meantime by accretion from the ranks of all who were most opposed to *capitulards* and *attentistes* alike. It remained, by process of natural selection, a band of men and women resolute and unwilling to compromise. But inclusion in its higher ranks of men who represented party-groupings on the underground front in France, or who had been closely associated with the parties of the Third Republic, gave it a different inner composition. It could fall, internally, into more politically recognizable strata once men like M. André Philip a Socialist, M. Georges Bidault a Catholic Democrat, and M. Louis Marin of the Right became eminent among its leaders.[2] It also

[1]*Speeches*, 11th November, 1942.

[2]De Gaulle, when he first negotiated with the underground movements, favoured a broad non-party political rassemblement: he soon changed his aim to one of an all-party alignment.

gave Gaullism the claim to more organic connection and more systematic contact with public opinion inside France; which gave it a new basis of authority and a stronger title to be representative of the French people than it had had before, or than the ex-Vichy authorities ranged behind Giraud could ever pretend to have. General Giraud's position, being inherently ambiguous and anomalous, could not indefinitely withstand the claims of such a movement, for it had none of the Resistance dynamism.

Giraud's authority rested on a somewhat fictitious apostolic succession of credentials from Pétain via Darlan. It sufficed to salve the consciences of the conservatively minded military and naval officers, civil servants and colonial administrators who found any transference of allegiance acutely embarrassing and perplexing. But it could not grow. It was Darlan, claiming to act on behalf of Pétain, who had first appointed Giraud as Commander-in-Chief; it was the Imperial Council, set up by Darlan and composed of Pétain's nominees as Governors-General, which on Darlan's death appointed Giraud High Commissioner for North Africa. The assumption underlying his position was endorsement of the legitimacy of Darlan's authority; its consequence was association with ex-Vichy officials. Both were absolutely repudiated by Gaullism. For a time in the winter of 1942 it looked as if France was to have two leaders, de Gaulle in London supported by Great Britain, and Giraud in North Africa supported by the United States. It was arranged that they should meet at Casablanca, and the world was presented with a carefully arranged photograph of them stiffly shaking hands.

At last a new French Committee of National Liberation was set up in June, 1943. The great weakness of this Algiers Committee was its consistent duality. It had, at first, both Generals as Presidents, and they were to preside alternately. Its membership was equally mixed. Giraud, whilst still protesting that he was no politician, in fact held the authoritarian conservative views which are normal to service-chiefs who regard themselves as "non-political". At first, too, both were Commanders-in-Chief. But once a merger of the two bodies had been achieved it was virtually inevitable that de Gaulle should triumph, that the more dynamic and revolutionary of the two wings of the Committee should, in a revolutionary situation, take the lead. Giraud was steadily and firmly ousted from political power, and relegated first to a purely military position and eventually to even a subordinate military capacity, with de Gaulle in supreme charge of both the political and military direction of the Committee. In November, 1943, a number of leaders of the resistance movements were included in the Committee. The Consultative Assembly was set up, and half its members represented the resistance movements inside France. In April, 1944, Giraud at last retired completely into private life, never to return. (He died in March, 1949.) In the Consultative Assembly the rank and file of the two movements got to know each other, learned to work together for the liberation of France, and the wounds caused by the events of November and December, 1942, were gradually healed. But it is noteworthy that it took some eighteen months, during which the resistance movements had to undertake the tremendous task of planning French participation in liberation, before the wounds were healed: eighteen months which might have been more profitably and economically spent by French leaders than in such prolonged jostling of each other. The "temporary expedient" which saved British and American lives did so at the expense of French energies and self-respect. The de Gaulle who emerged from this phase was a more wily, astute and experienced politician than the de Gaulle of London. His eviction of Giraud from power was a masterpiece of machiavellian tactics. In Algiers he underwent his apprenticeship in parliamentary and governmental techniques. It was a subtle and insidious school.

By the end of 1943, therefore, the National Committee had found some homogeneity and unity; it had reinforced its authority through the institution of the Consultative Assembly; it had been officially recognized by the rest of the United Nations. Under its rule in North Africa trade unions revived, Vichy laws were repealed and Vichy supporters removed from office, the Communist Party was allowed to come into the open and publish its paper *Liberté*. The Committee soon became, both in claim and in substance if not in name, the Provisional Government of France, even before D-Day. General de Gaulle could declare, amidst the applause of the Consultative Assembly, that "the French Committee of National Liberation is in fact the government of the French Republic". It was at least a shadow-government, and it set about preparing to take over actual provisional administration of metropolitan France after liberation. That the new regime should be in form parliamentary was made more probable by the authority won by the Consultative Assembly in Algiers. The Committee looked more and more to it to furnish that basis of moral authority and popular approval which it most needed. De Gaulle summed up the relationship between Committee and Assembly like this: "This support brings to it, first, greater national authority to justify and mobilize against enemies and traitors all the forces of the nation. This support allows it to have, in the concert of free peoples, greater authority and wider hearing for our service to the common cause. This support, finally, is overwhelming proof that democracy, to whose laws we have been faithful and which we are now restoring in practice, is identical with the highest interests of France." The Assembly, during the spring of 1944, established a degree of ascendancy and control over the Committee which was very inadequately suggested by its title of "Consultative" Assembly. It criticized policy, it passed resolutions, it insisted on inquiring into how far its "advice" had been taken, and in short behaved increasingly like a real parliament. Whilst Darnand and his collaborationist militias were forcing civil war in France, the Assembly clamoured for more thorough "purification" of the North African administrations, and criticized the inadequacy of the Committee's rather formal and legalistic outlook for the realities of a revolutionary situation. It was a case of the Jacobins ousting the *Feuillants* all over again. But even the formidable immediate tasks did not prevent the laying of more long-range plans. The idea which later bore fruit as the French Union was mooted in the early months of 1944 by M. Lapie in the Consultative Assembly. Individuals, too, like M. Vincent

Auriol, won their future official eminence in the Fourth Republic by their activities in the preparatory debates in Algiers. Decisions, such as the extension of the vote to women, and the resolve to hold early general elections after liberation, were also reached long before the expulsion of the Germans from French soil. From the earliest stages in the genesis of the Fourth Republic it was General de Gaulle who presided over its creation. He, more than any other person, was the midwife of the Fourth French Republic.

Was this the attainment of that "new power" which de Gaulle had originally mentioned in October, 1940, in his broadcast from Brazzaville? It must be noted that the whole conception of a "Fourth Republic" was by no means new. In the years between the wars several proposals had been made for a revision of the Third Republic radical enough to justify its renumbering. Jean de Granvillers had urged a "Fourth Republic" with plebiscitary foundations; Marcel Déat and Jacques Doriot, both to become extreme collaborators of the Germans, had equally clamoured for a new more authoritarian and a less parliamentary "Fourth Republic". The very phrase, and the concepts of a revolutionary breach with the parliamentary traditions of the pre-war regime which it implied, thus had ill-omened associations. It may be sensible and natural to number monarchs, but it becomes slightly absurd to go on numbering Republics. Yet de Gaulle and his followers deliberately favoured this notion, presumably because it chimed with their essentially revolutionary impetus. The subsequent Gaullist *Rassemblement* would, as some of its members have said, prefer a "Fifth Republic" to replace the Fourth.

* * * * *

Before considering his influence on the new Republic, it is necessary to notice the influence of the revolutionary situation on his own character and outlook. The course of events after 1940 forced all French leaders of resistance to go behind the forms of constitutionalism and the principles of the rule of law, and to seek authority from the fountain-head of French national will—popular sovereignty. They turned inevitably to traditionally Jacobin ideas of the "general will", as described by Jean-Jacques Rousseau and as transformed in practice by the French Revolution. They concluded that the "general will" of the French people exercised its "national sovereignty" directly through organized resistance to the German invader, and by proxy through loyalty to the cause of Gaullism and to the French National Committee. The Committee claimed to serve as temporary trustee for French interests internationally. It was less a matter of restoring democracy to France than of restoring France to democracy. This could be achieved only through a momentous act of national will, which would create a new political order. This moment had to be prepared for in Algiers by provisional plans and firm leadership. It all involved a theory not of parliamentary constitutionalism, not of the rule of law, not of direct continuity with republican legality and the Third Republic: it was essentially a theory of revolutionary Jacobinism. And it was a theory which General de Gaulle, both by reason of his position as the focus of Gaullist *mystique* and by his grasp of the actual situation, fully adopted and endorsed. He acted on the notion of an implicit mandate from the French people, and regarded it as his task to canalise this popular will through the Consultative Assembly, to provide a vehicle for it through the National Committee. He told the Consultative Assembly, on 27th March, 1944, "Some speakers have referred . . . to the importance which the attitude and decisions of the Assembly and the Government might have abroad. The Government begs you to take account only of what emerges from the will of the nation, of that and nothing else." In his public speeches and pronouncements he increasingly adopted the vocabulary and jargon of the Jacobin demagogue, and there is not the slightest reason to doubt his sincerity in so doing. The Cross of Lorraine was now inscribed with the ideals of "Liberty, Equality, Fraternity": Joan of Arc held hands with Maximilian Robespierre.

The strength of left-wing movements amongst the resistance groups encouraged this attitude. By personal inclination it seems likely that de Gaulle favoured the Catholic Democrat outlook which later found expression in the *Mouvement républicain populaire* (M.R.P.). But he was anxious to work and to reach agreement with Socialists and Communists alike as far as he could. In April, 1944, he introduced two Communists, MM. Billoux and Grenier, into the Committee as Commissioner of State and Commissioner for Air, but he made himself "Chief of the Armed Forces". By including Radicals and Socialists in the Committee as well as Communists, he completed the process of conversion into an all-party organization. It was preparation for D-Day, and he accompanied it by an appeal to the French people to subordinate all personal, group and party interests to the cause of national unity at the impending moment of supreme crisis. He planned for civilian and military Commissioners, appointed by the National Committee, to operate in France immediately the allied landings began. On 15th May, 1944, the Assembly unanimously resolved that the National Committee be re-christened the "Provisional Government of the French Republic". But just when preparations appeared to be going well, and the moment of liberation approached, relations between de Gaulle and his allies suddenly reverted to their bad old habit of cross-purposes and bickering. In the event, General de Gaulle did not land in France on D-Day, alongside his allies.

At the end of May Mr. Churchill announced that General de Gaulle had agreed to come to London "to talk things over", but he reaffirmed that Great Britain could not treat the French Committee of National Liberation as "the full, final and lawful embodiment of the French Republic". It was evident that de Gaulle had forced the pace too fast, in claiming to be head of the "Provisional Government of the French Republic". The Committee already enjoyed a limited *de facto* recognition by the United States and Great Britain, and—since August, 1943—recognition by the Soviet Union "as representing the State interests of the French Republic". The United States, most reluctant of all to give formal recognition diplomatically, merely recognized the Committee "as administering French territories overseas which recognize its authority". It had been hoped that de Gaulle's meeting with Mr. Churchill at Marrakesh in January, 1944, would reach a *détente*, but apart from economic arrangements it did not. The allies were, in short, confronted with the claim of de Gaulle to represent not, as in 1941, any continuity with the Third Republic; nor, as in 1942, to represent a *de facto* authority administering French territories; but to be the popularly supported trustee for French national sovereignty and therefore the only proper provisional government of France during the period of liberation. This would mean that internally it would assume immediate responsibility for administering freed areas of metropolitan France, and that externally it would represent France in the councils of the allies. The doctrine of Jacobinism, so vital an element in the unified resurgence of France, brought obstacles to the smooth relationship between Gaullism and the United Nations. It raised the awkward question of legal diplomatic status, which was just the sort of issue on which de Gaulle was determined to reach no compromise: it raised all the old suspicions on both sides. The allies felt that they had been "bounced": de Gaulle felt that he had been "let down". And all this a week before D-Day. It was October, 1944, before the Provisional Government received formal recognition by the allies: some two months after the liberation of Paris and the installation of the Gaullist Government in France.

The responsibility for this unhappy chain of incidents is difficult to place precisely. Certainly the United States' sponsoring of Darlan and Giraud, like their lenient treatment of Vichy before that, bedevilled relations between de Gaulle and the major forces of liberation. The Soviet Union and even Britain would both have been more ready than the State Department to accord de Gaulle's Committee formal diplomatic recognition much sooner. But it was clearly important to avoid any discord in allied action at so critical a moment, and the State Department was allowed to set the pace. On the other hand, the reasons for American reticence and caution were not unconnected with previous American experience of de Gaulle, and it is difficult to avoid his having to shoulder most of the responsibility for the *impasse* into which his own relations with his major allies had fallen. His reputation as a reliable guide to French reactions did not stand high after Dakar, and his high-handed habits in dealing with his allies showed that he had failed to realize that one in his own oddly isolated eminence could never be forgiven mistakes of judgment. It is hardly likely that the United States hoped to repeat in France what it had carried through in North Africa—an initial deal with Vichy administrators which might lighten allied losses and ease allied invasion. Much had happened inside France since 1942, and anyhow France had never been comparable to North Africa. Some of the General's more suspicious supporters feared, however, that this might be the American design, and the exaggerated xenophobic quality of their reactions did nothing to improve the position.

They failed to understand the point of view that even the National Council of Resistance did not represent the whole of "resistance"; that even it was not necessarily wholeheartedly behind de Gaulle and his colleagues; and that despite all efforts of de Gaulle to institutionalize his support inside France, there were many millions (including the prisoners of war in German camps) whose views none could yet predict. Allied reluctance to forestall the French national will was more reasonable than the Gaullists could allow: and the United States could claim to be more orthodoxly "Jacobin" in its attitude than de Gaulle.

It is alleged that, on 5th June, 1944, when de Gaulle left Algiers for London at Mr. Churchill's urgent request, because D-Day was on the morrow, the two old colleagues had the most violent quarrel of all. De Gaulle refused, it is said, to address a message to the French people at the same time as the other allied leaders, because he was not formally recognized by them. "Very well," said Churchill, "I shall say in the House of Commons that General de Gaulle refuses to associate himself with the greatest effort made to liberate France!" De Gaulle climbed down, but as he was not allowed to speak before General Eisenhower he spoke five hours later, broadcast instructions at variance with those already given by General Eisenhower, and refused to allow more than a small group of liaison officers to accompany the initial force of American and British invaders.[1] He himself arrived in France only on 14th June: eight days after D-Day and two days later than Mr. Churchill. On that day the British Prime Minister, replying to questions in Parliament on relations with the French National Committee, said, "I must advise

[1]Maurice Martin du Gard, *op. cit.*, pp. 373–4; H. de Kerillis, *op. cit.*, pp. 200–10; Dwight D. Eisenhower, *Crusade in Europe* (1948), p. 272; Harry C. Butcher, *My Three Years with Eisenhower* (1946), pp. 562, 570.

the House most seriously that a debate on this matter would have very great dangers." He added that, "In addition to our relations with the Committee we have also to consider our very close relations with the United States and their relations with the body I have just mentioned. I think it would be better to allow the relationships prevailing between General de Gaulle and the United States to proceed further before we have a formidable debate on these questions, which might well be of comfort to the enemy." As soon as Paris was freed, but not before, Britain signed an agreement for the taking over by the National Committee of the civil administration of liberated France, and General Eisenhower was authorized to treat with the Committee as the *de facto* authority in France "so long as they continue to receive the support of the majority of Frenchmen who are fighting for the defeat of Germany and the liberation of France." Hints and implications could not be clearer.

It was not that the allies expected to find in France any authority more representative or more popularly acceptable to the French people than the Gaullist Committee. But they felt, rightly or wrongly, that it was wise to avoid any suggestion of foisting an external authority upon the French nation, and to allow it to become abundantly clear from popular reactions that de Gaulle and his supporters were acceptable before they were accorded civil administrative power. They also feared lest any independent authority accorded to de Gaulle at so touchy a moment as the landing and early phase of liberation might be wilfully used, and might bring discord and confusion into allied action. "Being rude to the British" to prove to the French that he was not a British pensioner became militarily dangerous. The suspicions were mutual, and each bred the other, in a vicious circle. It was the nemesis of Carlton Gardens intrigue and Algerian squabbles. The Cross of Lorraine, it was remarked, was the heaviest cross that the British Prime Minister had to bear. Yet he bore it well.

One remarkable incident revived in an instant all the old *mystique* of Gaullism. On 26th August, 1944, it was arranged that Charles de Gaulle should walk at the head of his troops from the tomb of the unknown soldier under the Arc de Triomphe to the Cathedral of Notre Dame, to celebrate the liberation of Paris. Militiamen and fascists were still at large in Paris, and soldiers of the French Forces of the Interior were still hunting them down. There were shots at the procession in the Rue de Rivoli. De Gaulle marched on unperturbed. Even inside Notre Dame a few snipers continued to fire. The General marched unwavering down the aisle, with the whir of bullets echoing around the Cathedral. He survived untouched. In Paris, at least, Charles de Gaulle was the hero of the hour, as in so many ways he deserved to be; although his conduct in June, 1944, had been in deplorable contrast with his conduct in June, 1940.

In September the Provisional Government was reorganized to meet the new needs of actually governing liberated France. It announced that Pétain's so-called "French State" was now abolished, along with all its laws, and declared that "legally the Republic has never ceased to exist". The General broadcast the announcement that as soon as liberation of

French soil was complete and the prisoners home again general elections would be held on universal suffrage of all men and women. Wherever he went he struck the note that the war-effort of France and her triumphant resistance had earned her the right to be heard in the settlement after the war; she must assert her due place in the United Nations. His aim was twofold: to restore confidence and a sense of purpose to French life; and to see that full account should be taken of French claims and French interests in any settlement with Germany and Italy, and eventually with Japan. It was in no small measure due to his efforts and persistence that France came to be accepted as one of the "Big Five" at San Francisco and within the structure of the United Nations Organizations. This almost unrecognized triumph of de Gaulle, a triumph because it was in the end achieved so silently, must be recorded amongst the greatest of his services to France.

By the end of 1944 most of the initial difficulties had been removed, and better relations began to prevail between the now fully recognized Provisional Government and its allies. When General de Gaulle entertained Mr. Churchill in Paris in November, after together taking the salute of the allied forces in the Champs-Élysées, they ostentatiously paid each other public compliments. Churchill added the impish remark: "Happily you have at this moment an uncontested chief. I have from time to time had some lively discussions with him, but I am sure you ought to rally round your chief and do your utmost to have France united and indivisible." Churchill at the same time agreed to a French zone of occupation in defeated

Germany, and to the demilitarization of the Saar, where control of the mines would be in French hands.

* * * * *

Between the liberation of Paris and the collapse of Germany de Gaulle did succeed in establishing France as one of the "Big Five". But it was not without difficulty. The problems of the Levant still deeply embroiled France and Britain, and by the end of May Churchill had intervened in a personal message to de Gaulle. "In view", he wrote, "of the grave situation which has arisen between your troops and the Levant States and the severe fighting which has broken out we have, with profound regret, ordered the Commander-in-Chief, Middle East, to intervene to prevent a further effusion of blood, in the interests of the security of the whole Middle East, which involves communications with the war against Japan. In order to avoid collision between British and French forces we request you immediately to order the French troops to cease fire and to withdraw to their barracks. Once firing has ceased and order has been restored we shall be prepared to begin tripartite talks here in London." Because the text of this message was read by Mr. Eden in the House of Commons, de Gaulle issued a public reply, and at a press conference two days later claimed that the French order to cease fire had been given a day before Churchill's note reached him. He blamed British interference for the troubles in Syria and Lebanon. "Deep friendship", he said, "unites the French and British peoples, but we must finish with dictates and crises." Three days later Mr. Churchill replied in the Commons to these

of France's painful recovery of a working structure of everyday social and economic life is beyond our present scope. It is true that the Provisional Government did miss opportunities in economic reconstruction: but that France did achieve so much recovery, even before German surrender, is no small tribute to the wisdom and skill of the ministers whom de Gaulle chose to serve him.[1]

The end of the war with Japan in September, 1945, and the end of the provisional regime which was reached when general elections to a Constituent Assembly were held in October, 1945, marked the opening of a new phase in the career of de Gaulle, as well as a new era in the history of France. Internationally he now swung over to the notion of Franco-British entente as a basis for a union of western Europe. Better relations had been established with the United States, Russian designs in eastern Europe were beginning to show themselves, and de Gaulle seems at this point to have decided to back western union. On 9th September he gave an important press-conference in which he surveyed Anglo-French relations and emphasized all that the two countries have in common. He explained that "despite the development of aviation and the discovery of the atomic bomb, western Europe constitutes a natural complex, the areas of which together could produce the means of livelihood in sufficient quantities to form an economic aggregate". He thought that though it

[1]There is little substance in the charge of Kerillis (*op. cit.*, p. 240) that it was foolish to put a former exile (Adrien Tixier) at the Ministry of the Interior, and a former underground resister (Georges Bidault) at the Ministry of Foreign Affairs. Both performed their tasks tolerably well. There is more substance in the charge that the Provisional Government neglected the monetary problem at this time.

would not be economically self-sufficient it need not be inferior to "other economic masses". That he was led to this emphasis by the urgent need to reach a settlement of the German problem in conformity with French interests of security became clear in the rest of his interview. He realized that French claims on the Rhineland, the Ruhr and the Saar could be met only as part of a wider settlement of western Europe. It was a shrewd and wise move in foreign policy, and shows his progress as a more realistic foreign statesman. He was gaining stature with experience.

He went on to develop this conception in subsequent speeches. A month later he visited Brussels and on his return spoke of the "western family", remarking that "a western organization does no harm to a European organization, and a European organization does no harm to a world organization". He spoke kindly of Italy, as "our Mediterranean neighbour—our cousin". He made a barter agreement with Czechoslovakia. The next five years were to prove that he had backed the right horse in the international stakes. One by one other western European countries came round to the same conception. De Gaulle must be given credit for being, in this respect, one of the most percipient national leaders in 1945.

Internally, the October elections produced a Constituent Assembly in which the three major parties—almost equal in strength—were the Communists, Socialists and M.R.P. (Catholic Democrats). The Assembly had seven months of life, during which it had to draft a new Constitution and submit it to a popular referendum. On 13th November this Assembly unanimously proclaimed de Gaulle head of the

Provisional Government. He was charged with constituting a Ministry acceptable to the Assembly. The Communists demanded one of the three key posts of Foreign Affairs, the Interior, and War. De Gaulle refused to give them any of these, offering instead four important economic portfolios. In a broadcast explaining the ministerial deadlock he showed plainly his realization of the link between domestic and external politics. "While I was fully disposed to admit the men of the party in question to the economic and social work of the Government, and to give them appropriate portfolios, I could not see my way to concede to them any of the three posts that determine foreign policy—diplomacy, which expresses it, the Army, which supports it, and the police which covers it. By acting differently . . . I would have risked not being able to answer—even in appearance, and in our tense universe appearances count a lot—for the French policy of equilibrium between two very great Powers, a policy which I believe to be absolutely necessary in the interests of the country, and even in the interests of peace." Foreign policy he regarded as a matter reserved for himself. Having failed to fulfil the mandate of the Assembly to form a Government of national unity he was—he explained—handing back that task to the Assembly. "If the Assembly decides to call on someone else to direct the affairs of the country I shall leave without bitterness the post in which, for five years and five months, in a period of the gravest peril in the history of France, I have tried to serve the country well."

On 19th November the Assembly, by 400 to 163 votes, charged him again to serve as head of the

Government, forming a three-party Ministry with the posts equitably distributed. In the event five Communists entered the Ministry, holding the key economic ministries of National Economy, Industrial Production, Armaments, and Labour, with M. Thorez as a Minister of State. The General thus goes down in French history as the first political leader to admit Communists to high ministerial office, as well as the first to extend the vote to women.

The programme enunciated on behalf of this tripartite Ministry included the nationalization of credits, electricity and insurance; reform of administration and the public services; and promotion of the physical, cultural and moral welfare of the people. It was accepted that reconstruction even on a drastic scale could not await the settlement of the constitutional framework. The Provisional Government had to provide for much else besides a new Constitution. Externally, he continued to repeat the broad principle that France would try to serve as a bond between east and west, and would try to keep an equilibrium between east and west; but in no circumstances would she allow herself to be a pawn of either. He saw her best function as a focal part of a western European organization. In December he reached final agreement with Great Britain about Syria and Lebanon. It provided for the systematic joint withdrawal of forces, so that complete withdrawal should be reached by both simultaneously. He made a trade agreement with the Soviet Union. France gained membership of the Far Eastern Commission. Things had taken a turn for the better once more, and the Provisional Government was shaking down remarkably well. The rhythm of interludes of good relations succeeded by periods of acute stress and tension seemed to have become almost normal.

* * * * *

In January, 1946, he announced suddenly that the conditions in which he was expected to lead the Government had proved impossible, and he had resolved to resign. He gave no clear reason why he had chosen this particular moment for his resignation. He reminded the country that he had led it towards "liberation, victory, and sovereignty", and oddly suggested that the critical period was over. The Socialist, Félix Gouin, succeeded him as head of the Government and within four days formed a new Ministry. It was the mixture as before, and Gouin announced that he would follow the same lines of foreign policy as de Gaulle. The General retired into private life, to a hunting-lodge in Marly Forest, leaving friends and critics alike to debate what was the balance of considerations which had determined his departure. It was an oddly abrupt and apparently inconsequential action, typical of so many of his actions during the war. It was suggested that he was disgusted with the irresponsibility and lack of solidarity of the parliamentary parties; that he disapproved of the new draft Constitution then being devised; that he could not agree to any reduction in the army estimates. None of these explanations provided a reason why he should be so enigmatic about his departure. So it was also suggested that his retirement was a tactical move, intended to allow him to return later by popular acclaim on more authoritarian terms; that he planned to exploit the deadlock into which he believed the parliamentary parties were inevitably drifting; that the shades of Bonapartism had not entirely receded from French politics.

The main consequence of his resignation was, however, plain enough. His own prestige sharply declined, and the draft Constitution of the Fourth Republic was, in the event, devised and presented to the people, in May, 1946, without Charles de Gaulle taking any direct share in its fate. It was rejected by the referendum, and a new Constituent Assembly had to be elected the following month. Meanwhile government by compromise and negotiation again became the rule. Watching this tedious process from his retirement, the General found that he could not sustain the aloofness which, in January, he had indicated he would adopt.[1] In the middle of June, he began to stump the country, making a series of great speeches at well-attended meetings. His central theme was an attack on the political parties, and on the type of Constitution which they were engaged in devising. At Bayeux he urged that France's new institutions should offset her tendencies to political deadlock by providing for stability and strong leadership. There must be a continuity above fluctuating political combinations—by which he meant a President of the Republic with real authority and power. Executive power should emanate from him, not from the legislature, which should be bi-cameral. The French

[1] I have been assured by his friends that this decision to "leave his tent" was preceded by a *crise de conscience* which lasted at least a week, and that only an urgent sense of duty eventually determined him to re-enter the fray. He certainly saw in the rejection of the draft Constitution a chance to exert influence on the next attempt, and regretted his over-hasty "retirement".

Union should be rebuilt on federal principles. Speaking at Bar-le-Duc he returned to the idea of an Anglo-French nucleus for a western European organization which might hold the balance between "the two new worlds of Russia and the U.S.A." By August he was attacking the second draft Constitution then emerging from the debates of the Second Constituent Assembly, and repeated his "Bayeux programme". He referred to himself as "a man who seeks no mandate, no function and no post", and posed as the disinterested friend of France, proffering her advice and warnings against the machinations of the parliamentary parties. It became clear how events were turning when the *Union gaulliste*, formed at first by René Capitant without de Gaulle's auspices to fight the coming elections, in mid-September received his official support. Its declared aim was to defeat the new draft and to press for the "Bayeux Constitution", with a strong Presidency and an executive independent of the legislature.[1] He regarded the new draft as substantially the same as the old—which was quite true—and advised the country to reject it. He spoke at Épinal at the end of September, and elaborated in more detail his vision of the Constitution. "The executive, legislative and judicial authorities must be separate and limited each to their functions." The head of the State should stand above parties and represent the unity of France and of the French Union. Parliament should make laws and supervise the Government, but should not itself try to govern.

[1]René Capitant published *Towards a Federal Constitution* (1946) as a sort of official Gaullist commentary on the "Bayeux Constitution". Its chief feature was an overwhelming concentration of power in the hands of the President.

Nor should the executive power proceed from the legislative; it should be dependent upon the head of the State. He insisted that these views were neither of the Left nor the Right, and for the first time adopted the royal "we" throughout his speech. He continued his attacks on the new draft Constitution up to almost the eve of the poll.

In November the draft was submitted to referendum and was accepted by 53.6 per cent. of those who voted. But nearly a third of the electorate (as against only one fifth in May) abstained from voting. "All Gaul," it was remarked, "is still divided into three parts; those who say reluctantly yes, those who say unconditionally no, and those who just don't care a damn." Thus a majority of the voters had not heeded de Gaulle's advice to vote against it; but there is little doubt that the high proportion of abstentions, which now made it possible to argue that the Constitution had been carried through by only a minority of the whole country, was largely due to his campaign against it. The effect of his efforts was, therefore, to prolong the period of discontent with the constitutional arrangements of the Fourth Republic. It took the next four years of persistent experiment and effort by the parliamentary parties to demonstrate to the country that the much-abused Constitution could in fact work, however uneasily. The nation, as Léon Blum remarked, was moving "from the provisional to the precarious".

At the end of 1946 interest began to focus on election of the first President of the Republic, who under the Constitution was accorded little more power than his predecessors of the Third. General de Gaulle made it known that he would not stand as a candidate, because "the exclusivist regime of the parties . . . cannot solve the very serious internal, imperial and external problems on which our whole life depends." The Socialist M. Vincent Auriol was elected President of the Republic. That spring de Gaulle missed no opportunity, whether in unveiling a memorial at Bruneval or in commemorating the liberation of Alsace at Strasbourg, to urge collaboration with Britain and the United States and to condemn the unstable ministerial system which the Constitution had perpetuated. His criticisms of the Communists, whom M. Ramadier was strong enough to eject from his Ministry in May, sharpened in tone. At Strasbourg he pointed out how, when parties had revived after liberation, "the disturbing and exceptional ambitions, tactics and methods of one of them compelled the others to adopt a similar form of organization". By sharing government among themselves the parties had, in consequence, produced paralysis. He offered an interpretation of his retirement in January, 1946. So long as there had been urgent tasks of war and reconstruction he had tried to form some kind of all-party national union. When party separatism became too strong he had been confronted with the dilemma of joining one of them or withdrawing altogether; he had withdrawn so as to avoid "a devaluation of the national capital".

This Strasbourg speech, made on 7th April, 1947, was paradoxically the prelude to the foundation of a party of his own. He declared, "It is time for the French people to rally and organize itself so that a great effort for the common weal and the reform of the

State can triumph and so that the French Republic can build a new France." A week later it was announced that he had put himself at the head of a new "Rally of the French people" (*Rassemblement du Peuple Français*). Its aim was "to advance and victoriously achieve, over our dissensions, the unity of our people in the tasks of renewal and reform of the State". He called for support from "all French men and women who mean to unite for the common weal, as they did yesterday for the liberation and victory of France". He insisted that the Rally was not a new political party, but a framework for the growing feeling of a common spirit and a desire for national unity above and apart from the parties. The relics of the old *Union gaulliste* joined it *en masse*. At the end of May the new movement held its first national congress. The General repeated to it his now familiar arguments. He added the significant remark that he had so far abstained from force and given the parties their chance, but that it was now clear that they could produce only dissension and futility. It was a time of widespread labour unrest, of strikes and great trade-union and Communist activity. To speak thus in an atmosphere of public disorder was ominous. Many began to feel that a new General de Gaulle was emerging, in a manner somewhat reminiscent of Colonel de la Rocque a decade earlier.[1]

As the Communist menace increased during the summer and autumn of 1947, de Gaulle came out more and more positively as a critic of the Soviet

[1]Jacques Debû-Bridel has written a well-informed but highly favourable account of the beginnings of the R.P.F. down to 1948 in *Les Partis contre Charles de Gaulle* (1948). He is a member of the *bureau* of the Rally's National Council and an avowed Gaullist. He was originally a *protégé* and ardent admirer of André Tardieu.

Union and of Communist tactics in France. In July he told the Anglo-American Press Association that Russian encroachments on European freedom could be checked only by an association of all nations in Europe which were "united by the spirit of freedom and of true democracy". He looked to close co-operation between France, Britain and the United States as the bulwark of freedom and peace. He likewise presented his own movement as the most hopeful bulwark against Communist advances inside France. At Rennes he condemned the threat to national unity from "a group of men whose leaders place subservience to a foreign State above all else"; and drew the moral that by resisting the "regime of impotence" into which Communist tactics had led the French party-system the R.P.F. was the only real guarantee of France's destiny. In this way he contrived to present to his audience the Soviet Union, the French Communist Party, and the unstable Constitution as inter-linked common enemies to French security which he alone proposed to withstand. It was astute propaganda, devised to grow in appeal and plausibility when the winter brought the great wave of strikes largely instigated by the Communist-controlled trade unions.

The rise of a movement claiming to stand above parties, appealing to ideas of strong leadership, and condemning alike Communism and parliamentary democracy was no new factor in French politics. Such phenomena had occurred often enough before in French history in unhappy circumstances, and usually with unhappy results. Some men saw in it a new threat to republican democracy, and in the

General a new Boulanger-de-la-Rocque.[1] Others recalled that it was in just this way that the Fascist and National Socialist Parties had risen to power between the two wars. So the movement started with powerful sales-resistance on the part of French public opinion. Soon, however, it became plain that the movement which had begun by posing as something above all parties was simply becoming another party. In August de Gaulle announced that the Rally would contest the municipal elections to be held in the autumn of 1947. The R.P.F. thus became merely a new party of the Right: and its leader, far from having withdrawn himself from political strife to avoid "a devaluation of the national capital", had decided to invest this capital in a party-cause. He came down into the arena of normal party politics and became almost permanently a politician on the stump, evolving a vocabulary of abuse peculiar to himself.

In October he spoke in Algiers and denounced the Communists—now habitually called "the separatists" —for undermining French authority in North Africa. He revived that most consistent of all themes in his career, devotion to the ideal of French imperial strength and unity. He remains, in every respect, an Imperialist. In the first round of the municipal elections the R.P.F. made sweeping victories, whilst the Communists lost ground heavily. The R.P.F. gained 38.4 per cent. of the votes, the Communists 30.6 per cent.; and in the Paris Municipal Council the R.P.F. won 52 out of the 90 seats. Its greatest gains were,

[1]The demands of General Boulanger, in June, 1888, for revision of the Constitution and for dissolution of the Chamber, were almost exactly repeated by de Gaulle at this time. De Gaulle has been accused, I think wrongly, of having belonged to the *Croix de Feu* of Colonel de la Rocque before the war.

significantly, in the larger towns, where the Communists had been most active. It came into strength, in short, on the rebound against Communism. De Gaulle followed up these electoral successes with a long pronouncement drawing the moral from them: there should be general elections, to provide a new Parliament with a mandate for constitutional revision and the erection of stronger government. The Jacobinism of liberation came uppermost again. "It is at its legitimate source, that is to say in the people's vote, that the indispensable authority needed by the Government of the Republic must, as a matter of urgency, be sought."

But during the winter of 1947–8 the Gaullists lost their first real opportunity. The Government—supported by the "Third Force" of those parliamentary parties which were equally opposed to Communism and to Gaullism—managed to survive and quell the great strikes without any aid from the R.P.F. The firmness of the Government combined with the good sense of the French workers brought a relatively peaceful return to work in most industries. The R.P.F. talked much but had no chance to do anything. It seemed that the Fourth Republic, in spite of its weaknesses, was tough enough to survive without the help of the extremists. And the growth of Western Union—a development which de Gaulle was compelled by his many past utterances to support—redounded to the credit of the parliamentarians, and began to form what was virtually an international "third force". All that he was left to do was to go on demanding early general elections: a demand not in itself very popular in a country which had known three general elections within the previous thirty months. But this he continued to do during the spring and summer of 1948, laying himself open to the accusations (which even those in the M.R.P. who were otherwise sympathetic to him, voiced) that he was trying to create "an artificial electoral fever in the country", when the real need was for economic reconstruction and a truce to constitutional squabbles. He found himself on a very bad wicket, and once again his political sense seems to have been faulty.

His propaganda had two great weaknesses at this time: he failed to make clear how, after new elections, he would contrive to rule above parties rather than through parties without adopting authoritarian methods; and his social and economic programme, at a moment when France's most urgent needs were clearly social stability and economic reconstruction, was vague in the extreme. In many of his previous speeches he had touched on proposed remedies for the country's economic ills. He proposed "association" between workers and employers. He hinted at the role of the State as arbitrator in economic disputes. He had supported the earliest steps in nationalization of key industries. In January, 1948, at St. Étienne, he explained that he believed that administration, management and men should settle their own wages and conditions of work; that representatives of the trade unions should be "incorporated in the State" (presumably in the second Chamber); and that the problem was a psychological one of getting away from the concept of class struggle and exploitation of workers by employers. These quite admirable sentiments could have been shared by many of his opponents, but offered no immediate practical programme and appeared too vague to win much support. It was felt that the man who knew so much about tanks did not necessarily know much about economics. But strikes went on through the summer, and cabinets went on collapsing or surviving for short periods by excruciatingly narrow votes of confidence. It might be that in the winter of 1948–9, when a further epidemic of great industrial unrest and strikes appeared probable, the Gaullists would be given a second opportunity to exploit the difficulties and disorder of the parliamentarians.

He began the autumn with a very distinct threat of force. The movement was indeed running away with its leader. At Grenoble, at Chambéry and at Annecy the General issued warnings that if elections were indefinitely postponed collapse might soon occur, and then he might "have to gather up the reins of authority" as he had done in 1940. The Government postponed the next batch of local (cantonal) elections from September until March. At Gaullist meetings in Paris and Le Havre there were clashes with Communists. In October de Gaulle told the press that if the Communists entered the Government all legitimate forms of government would come to an end, and he then "reserved his own rights to take future action". The expected epidemic of strikes began. The shadow of civil war loomed up over the horizon.

The Government, with the Socialist Jules Moch at the Ministry of the Interior, took more firm and drastic action than before. By November police and troops had taken over some of the main pits and power-stations, and the heart fell out of the strike movement.

Again, this time in spite of the General's open threats of force, the Gaullists had made no move, and the Government had shown that it could keep order by its own official means. Immediately, the Rally itself began to suffer on the rebound. Various political parties allied or associated with it began to fall away. De Gaulle tried to captivate some of his more right-wing supporters by a remarkable press-conference in March, 1949, in which he echoed several sentiments favourable to Vichy. Marshal Pétain, who was still living under a form of house-arrest, should be allowed to end his days in better conditions. Collaborators should be amnestied, because it was absurd that so many young men should be wasting away their days in prison when they might be usefully employed. Franco-German understanding was essential to the stability of Europe, and French defence could not hinge on England. Is clearer evidence needed that he was becoming indeed the captive of his own movement?

In the cantonal elections of March the Gaullists suffered a setback, although they gained 389 seats in all, as against 334 of the non-Gaullist conservative groups and only 37 of the Communists. Despite its survival, the Rally was no longer regarded as the main bulwark of conservatism; and the chief feature of the elections was the resurgence of the Radicals, the traditional party of the "little men" of France, whether farmers or traders. The creaking in the internal structure of the R.P.F. became audible. It carried out some reorganization. In June several Gaullists were arrested by the police when arms were discovered in two cars making for Paris. M. Moch announced in Parliament that they had been staging an absurd plot to overthrow the regime, and that they were mostly young men "nostalgic for the underground life they had led during the period of resistance". Colonel Delore, one of the conspirators, later committed suicide in prison. The next month M. Giacobbi, one of the most ardent of war-time resistance leaders, resigned from the chairmanship of the R.P.F. Parliamentary group, and from its executive council, in protest against the way in which it had abandoned its non-party character. Four Deputies, newly ejected from it, published an open letter warning de Gaulle of the increasingly "feudal" attitude of the Rally, and urging him to dismiss some of its leaders. It was perilously like the quarrels of the courtiers all over again, and the prestige of the movement declined sharply.

In September M. Henri Queuille celebrated the anniversary of his assumption of office—it was extraordinary for one ministry to have survived for a whole year. He issued a report on the material gains of the year, and emphasized that France had made remarkable economic recovery and achieved a degree of social and political stability greater than any since the war. The gains were genuine. Food prices had at last started to fall, and that was the ordinary man's test of any government's success. But within a week M. Queuille, too, had started to fall; and the resulting crisis, until M. Bidault formed a new cabinet, lasted some three weeks, which was the longest crisis yet in the experience of the Fourth Republic. General de Gaulle did not miss this opportunity. At Bordeaux he declared that it was a fallacy to believe that France had gained stability and security. Her economy was bolstered by Marshall Aid; the relation between wages and prices was still very far from satisfactory; and the burden of another war would still, in spite of British and United States support, fall upon an inadequately prepared France. This argument, and the charge that French interests in Germany were being neglected by Britain and the United States and insufficiently defended by the Government, remained the only platform on which he could now stand. And so the General and his Rally entered the year 1950 weaker than at any time since the formation of the R.P.F. As Communism receded, so Gaullism lost much of its *raison d'être.*

But Communism, though checked, had by no means been rendered harmless to France: and so long as it was a threat, Gaullism had some *point d'appui.* It can be argued that the setback of Gaullism at the cantonal elections of March, 1949, where they polled just over 26 per cent. of the total vote as against 40 per cent. in the municipal elections of October, 1947, means simply that the Gaullists were stronger in urban than in rural areas. Again, only half the cantons held elections in March, 1949, and they did not include the department of the Seine, where Gaullism tended to be strongest. On the other hand, there were signs that de Gaulle was losing grip over the popular imagination of the more stolid and substantial sectors of the electorate. His public speeches resorted more and more to a highly personal and grandiloquent vocabulary which disturbed many of his listeners. The revelations by the Minister of the Interior that the security measures which had to be taken at his rallies were costing the taxpayer extremely large sums of money told against him with the more thrifty, and were some evidence of the threat to public order which his movement constituted. French memories easily carried back again to the tactics of the pre-war militant leagues, which contrived to provoke the very disorders which they pretended to be so willing to prevent. Combined with these more topical factors on the debit side against him in 1950, were the traditional French distrust of a General in politics: the memories of a Pétain, a Boulanger, a Macmahon, and even a Bonaparte. There was no evidence that time was on the side of the General.

There were signs that he realized this. In mid-February, 1950, after some months of relative silence, he made a speech to a vast crowd in the Vélodrome d'Hiver in Paris. It was designed to exploit the latest ministerial crisis caused by the withdrawal of the Socialists from the Ministry of M. Bidault, and at the same time to prepare for battle in the general elections. It may serve as a convenient index of his attitude and policy in 1950. He killed rumours of a ministerial coalition between the R.P.F. and the M.R.P. by proclaiming that his Rally was prepared to enter into negotiations with other parties on how to bring about elections, but not on how to prolong the existing regime. He cast new light on his motives in retiring in January, 1946—an incident which he clearly felt increasingly compelled to explain away. The people then supported him, but all who were organized—Communists, Vichyists, the parties and the trade unions—opposed him. He had then the means to impose his will, but he had refused to do so because he was convinced that nothing durable could be created without the express will of the people, nor would French interests internationally have prospered after such a *coup d'état*. But although he had rejected dictatorship—a significant admission that such a possibility had even been considered by him in 1946—he could never become reconciled to the existing regime of parties. He had withdrawn to make possible the experiment with the party State. It had been made and had discredited itself. The party State, "drifting on an ocean of perils, can bring forth from within itself nothing but a Parliament without faith or hope, and Governments without character or credit". In the next elections the R.P.F. would give support only to those candidates who belonged to it: he did not preclude, apparently, co-operation with rival groups or parties after the elections. Attacking Communism and the growing menace of the Soviet Union, he pointed out—amidst the only whole-hearted applause of the evening—that the only force then actively resisting Russia was the French army in Indo-China. He appealed for support from three types of French idealism: from those concerned with the extension of social justice, from those anxious to maintain the national tradition, and from those preserving the Christian faith. He put particular emphasis on his social programme for association of capital and labour on a profit-sharing basis.

Both the principles and tactics of Gaullism in politics are evident enough from this speech. Charles de Gaulle was girding himself for electoral battle; he was devising a composite appeal to the strongest forces in French life outside the ranks of Communism; and he was planning, when general elections should come, to open yet a new phase in his career as a political leader. By June, 1950, when the R.P.F. held its annual congress in the midst of yet another ministerial crisis caused by the overthrow of M. Bidault's government, the movement could claim with considerable show of confidence that its time was coming. Labour unrest, nursed by the Communists, went on sporadically; British coolness towards the "Schuman Plan" for a pooling of the coal and steel production of western Europe left France with greater initiative; the outbreak of war in Korea brought the threat of world war nearer. Circumstances seemed to be turning in favour of an authoritarian nationalistic movement. The speech of de Gaulle on 26th June left no doubts about his readiness and resolve to exploit these circumstances to the full. Demands for the revival of a "Charlemagne Union", stretching from the Elbe to the Pyrenees, found new strength. Even a new "Emperor Charles" was waiting in the wings. France would clearly hear a great deal more of Charles de Gaulle.

* * * * *

The difficulty of reaching a true estimate of de Gaulle's character and of his significance in present-day France is that, like Pierre Laval, he has become a personality who arouses the most violent and contradictory passions. To those who have maintained their war-time adoration and hero-worship of him as the very heart of French national resistance his transformation into a party leader and a politician induces no failure of devotion. To them, as to himself, he is but fulfilling his manifest destiny and is still the Joan of Arc of our times. To others who, whatever may have been their views of him as a soldier and a resistance-chief, regard his metamorphosis into a politician as at best an error of judgment and at worst a menace to democracy in France, he has become a focus of fear and hatred. He is, to them, a fascist General of a familiar type, and his Rally is but an imitation and a repetition of those aggressively nationalistic and authoritarian movements from which nearly every country, including France, suffered a decade before. One British weekly—very unjustly—even published photographs of de Gaulle making speeches and receiving bunches of flowers from little girls, juxtaposed to corresponding photographs of Hitler doing these same things. His movement, being so essentially negative in its anti-Communism, anti-parliamentarianism, anti-Sovietism, drew into its ranks a strange medley of men and groups. Some of these at least are suspect of undemocratic intentions. It appeared from the start to be well financed, and sinister industrialists were mentioned as its backers. Even former supporters of Vichy, and men of the old extreme Right who until then had been politically eclipsed, began to find in the R.P.F. a secure and respectable vehicle for their own return to political life. De Gaulle started a band-waggon on which many oddly assorted characters hastened to climb with almost indecent haste. In addition, some of his old entourage who had done so much to discredit and embarrass him in London and Algiers still clung resolutely to his "court". Whatever the sincerity and intentions of the General himself, it could at least be argued that the forces rallied behind him were suspect and unsavoury; that there appeared to be every danger that he might become the captive of his own movement; that the band-waggon he had started might soon run out of control, and carry him along in directions in which he had no original or natural wish to proceed.

There is, then, a paradox in the whole evolution of de Gaulle which calls for careful analysis and explanation. The man whose whole eminence rests on his defiance of fascism and his utter refusal to countenance collaboration with Hitlerism, who has presided over the restoration of parliamentary democracy in France, who has been the first to extend ministerial power to Communists and political rights to women, is now detested by millions of his countrymen and is denounced as a fascist. De Gaulle cannot be understood at all unless this paradox can be removed.

What is the case that de Gaulle is a would-be despot? It can be argued that in raising the standard of revolt in 1940 he was making a bid for personal power; that his behaviour during the period of exile was autocratic and at times disastrously high-handed; that by his jealous monopolizing of leadership he did the cause of Free France as much harm as good, and that by his refusal to countenance co-operation with former Vichy supporters he did much to perpetuate and intensify civil strife in liberated France; that his experiment in presidential power, during the period of Provisional Government, demonstrated that the strong presidential executive power which he now urges worked no more satisfactorily than the normal parliamentary system; that his retirement from office, which he has admitted was the alternative to a *coup d'état*, was a mere device for biding his time in the manner of Louis Napoleon a century before; and that his emergence as leader of an allegedly "non-party" movement and as a popular demagogue thriving on anti-communism and anti-parliamentarianism is but a new stage in his deliberate quest for personal despotism. His career makes it plain that his temperament is autocratic, in spite of his actions in restoring parliamentary institutions, and that he does not easily tolerate rivals or even colleagues in wielding power. Men recall some of his more unfortunately authoritarian remarks in his praise of personal leadership in *Le fil de l'épée* of 1932. His actions since 1940 seem only too often to endorse these principles. His latter-day readiness to threaten violent action, and to proceed in a spirit of opportunism and tactical manoeuvre, suggests that whatever his original motives and designs may have been he had by 1950 made himself candidate for a personal concentration of authority which would not be reconcilable with parliamentary modes of government.

This case against de Gaulle, which is heavily supported by Muselier and by most of the parliamentary party leaders,[1] is cogent enough in itself to demand caution from even those who supported him in time of war and who admire his military achievements. The vagueness in his proposals as to how he would attempt to govern "above parties" adds fuel to these doubts. A presidential republic, based on the principles of separation of powers such as he urges,

[1]It has been stated very much more forcibly than here by, for example, H. de Kerillis, in *I Accuse de Gaulle*, and by Louis Rougier, *Mission secrète à Londres* (1945, new ed. 1946), Chap. 12. But there is a case against de Gaulle which does not need such revelry in scandals and gossip.

was attempted in 1848. Within three years it had produced the dictatorship of the president, in the form of the Second Empire of Napoleon III. The regime of Vichy, beneath its war-time emergency trimmings, was in essence an executive power not responsible to parliamentary assemblies. The period of Provisional Government, with de Gaulle as its chief, which prevailed between 1944 and 1945, was likewise a form of presidential regime, with an executive owing allegiance not to the Consultative Assembly but to its President. The arrangements which he urges have therefore been tried, in various forms, and have been found wanting. Frenchmen are not easily persuaded that a further experiment is desirable or more likely to succeed.

Nor do several other developments since liberation lull these fears and suspicions. His increasing tenderness to Vichy supporters, justified so far as it is a reaction against the extreme clamour for *épuration*, looks too much like an opportunist gesture towards certain elements now supporting the R.P.F. His fidelity to some members of his entourage, like Gaston Palewski and the famous "Colonel Passy" of the secret service, is open to criticism. As early as February, 1945, a body called the *comité de regroupement républicain* issued an appeal for "the active union of all patriots behind General de Gaulle", and this union was to preserve the "essential hierarchies". Two of its leaders, including its secretary, were men who had supported Colonel de la Rocque before the war. The attractiveness of de Gaulle for so many elements of the old Right, even when not cultivated deliberately by the General himself, was evident and strong enough to alienate all those whose instinctive distrust of a General in politics was reinforced by anxieties about his willingness to lend himself to such men. He has a talent, worthy of Charles I, for trusting those whom he should not trust, and for distrusting those whom he could trust. In the face of these developments and anxieties, de Gaulle's repeated attempts to explain away his abrupt "retirement" and his hasty return to political life, and his recurrent efforts to explain that he has no ambitions for personal power, do not sound convincing. Nor do they accord well with his veiled threats to use a force which there is no evidence he commands, save by his ability to foment civil disorder; threats directed, after all, against a Constitution which has been freely and democratically accepted in a popular referendum.

This is the case against de Gaulle. It is not entirely convincing because it tends—like so much of the usual case against Laval—to read history backwards, to seek a higher degree of consistency and deliberate foresight than it is reasonable to expect in any man. The interpretation suggested by this study is that no such far-reaching ambition or "plot" is credible: but that an explanation of the metamorphosis of de Gaulle must be sought and can be found in the sequence of events between 1940 and 1944. Thrown into a focus of remarkable eminence and hero-worship during these years, convinced both temperamentally and intellectually that he was, as Churchill dubbed him, a man of destiny with a mission to fulfil, his naturally egotistical and brooding nature evolved certain Napoleonic characteristics. He had always regarded military and political affairs as closely inter-connected. Each crisis in the long sequence of vicissitudes in his relations with his adherents, his allies and his opponents amongst former Vichy sympathizers served only to sharpen and intensify these tendencies. He was the man who survived every adversity, and whose star never failed him in the end. In the ultimate values his tragedy is precisely the same tragedy as that of Laval: the old Greek tragedy of *hybris*, or overweening pride. Had he been capable, in adversity, of showing towards others the same degree of forbearance and magnanimity that Winston Churchill showed towards him, he might have escaped from the tragic climax. But his fate becomes that of the man who won for himself in the hearts of millions of his countrymen an affection, a respect and an adoration such as only he himself could have destroyed. His position in French affairs in 1950 is the measure of how far he has gone along this tragic path.

The seeds of this development were, however, there from the first. We have seen how his writings have been as much concerned with politics and sociology and the psychology of leadership as with the techniques of warfare. Although he justly earned for himself an unrivalled reputation for originality and independence of mind as a military technician and an expert in mechanized modes of warfare, it would be quite wrong to depict him as at any stage the pure military technician. He saw military strategy and tactics, and even military recruitment, organization and training, as semi-political matters. He had a powerful bias towards politics and a strong interest in the social sciences from the very start. It was this bias which made the evolution of the soldier into the politician so easy: to him it seemed natural and indeed inevitable. He had, moreover, even in the stricter limits of his military studies, always been something of a rebel. His independence of mind was so strong that he was prepared to challenge, at every stage, the orthodox teachings of his superiors. Beginning as a revolutionary strategist, he became after 1940 a political revolutionary, and in the circumstances of French resistance a revolutionary of the Left, appealing to Jacobin traditions and ideals. Then, after 1945, he became—because of his own political frustration and his inherent temperamental bias—a revolutionary of the Right, challenging both Communism and parliamentary democracy. As always, having set his foot on the path of defiance, he found himself led into ever more extreme forms of defiance, even if it led him, like Laval, to move from Left to Right. There is a consistency and logic in his whole career, and the paradoxes are only superficial.

Writing in 1950 it would be rash to predict that de Gaulle has no political future in France. He is only 60, and the French tend to acquire an affection for even political Generals as they get older. The elements of instability, both political and economic, afford little basis for optimism or complacency about the future of the Fourth Republic. Communism remains strong and heavily entrenched in certain industries. The personal *mystique* which accrued to his name during resistance has never been utterly dissipated. He has the support of good men, like René Capitant and André Malraux. A succession of parliamentary scandals or ministerial crises could very quickly discredit the "Third Force". General elections must come, in 1951 if not sooner: and if the R.P.F. can hold together until then it might still prove capable of capturing a large vote in the towns.[1] All that can be done is to assess the future in terms of the evolutionary process by which the brilliant military technician and the inspiring resistance leader of the pre-war and war years has been transformed into the very much less brilliant and less inspiring political tactician of the post-war years.

Egotism and a boundless self-confidence are essential elements in his character. His career suggests that, when he has convinced himself of the righteousness of his cause, he will spare no energy and shirk no dangers to serve that cause. He is like Pierre Laval in at least one respect: he is capable of completely identifying his own domination with the good of his country as he conceives it. Such a man is always dangerous, though in moments of national crisis he may be indispensable. But his career also reveals certain inherent weaknesses of character as a political leader. He is impulsive and, in certain combinations of circumstances, wilfully wayward. He is liable to withdraw, in untimely fashion, into something remarkably like the sulks. He is prone to utter firm general pronouncements which he later finds himself unable to sustain. He is overtrustful of men who, so long as they obey him faithfully, are allowed to enmesh him in a network of unsavoury intrigues; and though he may not himself indulge or share in these intrigues, at least he is too tolerant of them. Nor is he entirely above actions which, to the outsider at least, are apt

[1]But 1951 will be the centenary of 1851, when President Louis Napoleon of the Second Republic established himself in power by *coup d'état* and overthrew the Republic: and Frenchmen have acute historical memories.

to appear perilously like personal treachery. He is, in short, an enigmatic character, a man of moods which are concealed by an impassive exterior, an introspective being whose actions, springing from prolonged inner cogitation, cause surprise and alarm to his colleagues because they have had no hint of the inner process which has produced them. Many of his weaknesses are the inevitable counterpart to his virtues: but there is some evidence that, as he has passed middle age in the peculiar conditions of eminence and power, his strong egotism—as so frequently happens—has come to predominate over those mystic qualities of heroism and self-sacrifice which first drew noble souls to him in the moment of supreme national distress. Retrospectively, too, he is as convinced that he was always right as he is convinced at any one moment that he is right. The spirit of repentance is lacking: and that is perhaps the most dangerous element of all in his spiritual make-up. Such a man can go very far in any nation where his rivals are hesitant or divided and public opinion is confused.

A man of destiny is the victim of his own character. Charles de Gaulle has committed himself to a course of political action which will surely work itself out to its inevitable conclusion. It is not in his character to retrace his steps, to admit an error, to go back on what he has committed himself to achieve. But that does not mean that he will achieve what he intends. The oldest drama of all is certain to work itself out to its end, as it did for Laval. Whether the consequences will be purely personal, or will involve the French people as a whole, the next few years will reveal.

Epilogue

THE COLLAPSE OF France in June, 1940, which was in so many respects the parting of the ways for Pierre Laval and Charles de Gaulle, posed a moral predicament. What, in the face of stark military defeat which leaves one's country helpless before the invader, is the duty of the true patriot? Is it his duty to make the best terms possible with the enemy before national disintegration can proceed further; to accept these terms, however harsh, and try to make the enemy abide by them; to use the time gained to improve one's position, to accumulate and nurse reserves of power and weapons of bargaining against the day when circumstances may become more favourable? Or is it to reject the very notion of defeat, to carry on the struggle, however meagre one's resources and however fearful the odds, to seek support and resources of resistance throughout the whole world, and venture all in an heroic struggle to the death which spurns all compromise? Each course has its dangers and its merits. The first is open to the insidious perils of defeatism, a sapping of the will to carry on the struggle for independent survival, a slow annihilation by an unscrupulous enemy. The threat of "polonization", of vicious terrorization and piecemeal extermination such as Poland endured at Nazi hands, was the constant threat should the experiment of Vichy fail. The second is open to the more obvious but equally drastic risks of total annihilation. It was only the preoccupation of German strength on other fronts, and especially on the Russian front, which saved the men of the *Maquis* from suffering even heavier losses than they did suffer: and had Britain, too, capitulated in the face of Nazi attack the heroic gesture of General de Gaulle would have proved in vain. Either course, therefore, throws one on the mercy of the decisions and powers of resistance of other nations. Neither course can secure independence in the short run, and either may lead to the regaining of independence in the long run. Nor is one reaction any less likely than the other to call for a high degree of self-sacrifice, human misery and ultimate heroism.

The choice between them depends less on calculations of prudence or of self-interest than on temperament. Experience offers contrary advice. Gambetta's *guerre à outrance* of 1870 failed: Stresemann's policy of "fulfilment" succeeded relatively well. The instinctive reaction of the technician in politics is to trust to *finesse*: the instinctive reaction of the technician in war, who really sees how the defeat has been caused, is to trust to the art of war. But the decisive factor in the final momentous act of faith is undoubtedly personal character and temperament. That is why the personal study of Laval and de Gaulle as men is the only ultimate clue to their parting of the ways in 1940.

As shown above, the first reaction of Laval, fully consonant with his previous career, was utter acceptance of defeat. He wished to make the best possible terms with Hitler. He wanted to push as many aces up his sleeve as he could. He hoped to find some *modus vivendi*, which he knew would be harsh, but which would nevertheless give France, with himself at her head, some place in the Hitlerian New Order which he believed was about to be triumphantly erected in Europe. He was ready, moreover, to resort to every device in his own vast repertoire of trickery and guile to exploit any and every concession which could be wrung from the enemy. As things turned out so much better than he had expected, as German difficulties and embarrassments multiplied, he contrived to find some equilibrium of forces which he could manipulate to his own—and his country's—fullest advantage. But having committed himself to staying in France, to accepting the armistice and defeat, he found himself enmeshed in a tangle of conflicting forces pulling in opposite directions and varying in strength with each new phase of the world war. In the end, too compromised with resistance to German pressure to retain favour with the Nazis as against the extremist collaborators, and too compromised with collaboration to hope for mercy from the resisters, he went down to his doom.

The first reaction of General de Gaulle, again fully consonant with his previous career, was utter rejection of defeat. Having known all along the way to resist Hitler, he sought new allies and new opportunities for carrying out his art of war. Believing that the German attempt at European and even world domination was doomed, and that therefore the time of German defeat must ultimately come when France would need to show her own contribution to liberation, he resolved to place himself at the head of resistant France. But soon he, too, found himself enmeshed in a tangle of conflicting political forces. He found the task of co-operating smoothly with his

British and American allies little easier than Laval found his task of reaching a *modus vivendi* with Hitler. His supporters, because they were by self-selection the most defiant of Frenchmen, were by no means easy to control. His own haughty and aloof temperament made this task none the easier. His position as an exile made him abnormally sensitive to points of national and personal dignity which his hosts and allies, so fully preoccupied with war, found at times irritating and at others intolerable. As with Laval, conditions and the course of events came more and more to dominate him and the fate of his policy.

Each having chosen his course, it soon came to seem that there could never be any form of reconciliation between them, or between the forces in French social life which they led. But "never" is a dangerous word to use in politics, as de Gaulle learned when he proclaimed that he had decided to withdraw from political life. And the tenderness shown by de Gaulle towards Marshal Pétain and collaborationists in prison, even if he did not show it until some five years after liberation, is perhaps some indication of how political gulfs can be bridged. The gulf between those who were for four years subjected to the rule of Vichy and the pressure of the German occupation, and those who, in exile or from French territories overseas, supported de Gaulle in continuing the war, is one of the most tragic cleavages in French life. As the tide of events forced more and more active resisters in France to look to de Gaulle as their focus of loyalty, there might have been some hope—given different personalities at the top—that the supporters of Vichy in its policy of obstructionism and the supporters of de Gaulle in his policy of resistance might have come to see some little merit in each other. That very few of them did so was because Vichy, in its death-throes, became so closely dominated by the extreme collaborationists, whilst the Gaullists became increasingly adamant against any form of reconciliation with the Vichy supporters. That this happened is due, above all, to the actions and characters of Laval on the one hand and of de Gaulle on the other. Laval was so ill-trusted and so utterly detested, de Gaulle was so absolutist and exclusive in his conception of what constituted resistance, that even the faintest hope of speedily bridging the gulf disappeared. Had de Gaulle acquired earlier some of Laval's political adroitness and perception, the fate of France after liberation would have been different. Either might have prevented the course of events from dominating so completely his life and his policy. But human character is what it is, and it would be as unreasonable to expect men of such sharply contrasting character to escape from their own mental and moral make-up as to have expected personal and sectional passions not to be enflamed after liberation. In these ways the story as a whole has all the elements of the greatest tragedy. It is not possible, as the career of Laval has shown, for a *politique* to breed a *mystique*. It is easy, as the career of de Gaulle has shown, for a *mystique* to become a *politique*.[1]

[1]Charles Péguy wrote: "The *mystique* for which men die becomes the *politique* by which men live." The process cannot be reversed, for "*tout commence en mystique et tout finit en politique*." That some militant supporters of Gaullist resistance felt the need for reconciliation between Vichy and "Free France" is shown by the eloquent book of Lucien Galimand, *Vive Pétain! Vive de Gaulle!* (1948), which expresses a moderate point of view too seldom expounded in Gaullist circles.

It would be completely misleading to think of either Laval or de Gaulle as "representative men". It is impossible to point to any permanent forces in French life, to any schools of thought or to any traditions of national action, which either of them in a strict sense "represents". Each is too completely an individual, and each too unusual an individual, to represent more than himself.[1] Each, indeed, is a unique character, with all the fascination and genius of the unique individual person, and to inflate them (or rather to obliterate them) into representing impersonal forces or factors would be to miss the whole point about them. Yet because they have played so crucial a part in great events the very contrasts between them illuminate some of the *nuances* of French political life under the Fourth Republic.

The most striking of these contrasts is the way in which Laval, at first identified with a party, increasingly detached himself from organized party affiliations, whilst de Gaulle, at first outside party connections and striving hard to keep above them, has nevertheless ended by close identification with a new party of his own. Each was ready to work with any and every group which would lend him support: but each distrusted self-immersion in the activities of one party, and showed a strong preference to stay poised above all parties, controlling and sustaining an equilibrium between opposing political forces.

[1] I cannot agree with Dr. Alfred Cobban's verdict (*The Cambridge Journal*, February, 1949, p. 284) that "He will keep his place in the history of our time as a symbol rather than as an individual", and that "It is difficult to believe that he exercised a decisive influence at any point". But, as stated below, it is certainly true that "the fundamental thing in Laval was the pacifism that was typical of a generation which, sickened by the wasted sacrifices of one world war, by an over-anxious desire to buy peace at any price, purchased a second war and still paid the price".

This discontent with the French parliamentary groups, and the attempt to escape from them, reflects a powerful trend in French political life which is too often overlooked. At the same time, each man represents, in his own character and career, a feature of the parties which explains this flight from party government. The sort of subtle, fluctuating group formation which was the political milieu most congenial to the manoeuvres of Pierre Laval condemned the governments of the Third Republic to chronic instability and sordid political bargaining. The sort of powerfully organized party, basing itself on a more rigid ideological foundation, which has emerged under the leadership of Charles de Gaulle has equally condemned the Fourth Republic to instability and ministerial deadlock. It has been the destiny of each man to carry these tendencies of his time to their extremes. Laval resorted to the ultimately indivisible splinter group of political action, one individual—himself, the most manoeuvrable and subtle of all. De Gaulle created the ideological party to end all parties—the "Rally of the French People". If it be a sign of greatness in a man to seize upon the inherent tendencies of his time and to press them to their final culmination, then both Laval and de Gaulle have earned the title of greatness: and even this tendency to carry any principle to its "logical" extreme is in itself a recurrent characteristic of French national development.

Nor, perhaps, is it fanciful to see in the widest divergences of outlook between them a personal embodiment and symbolization of the extremes of attitude which generate so much tension in French life. The pacifist, insular, provincial outlook of Laval is one pole: the expansionist, imperialist, grandiose and world-wide horizons of de Gaulle form the other pole. Between these poles French policy has been stretched for the past two or three generations. The civilian, parliamentarian, materialistic mode of thought of Laval is one extreme: the militarist, authoritarian, dogmatic mode of thought of de Gaulle is the other extreme. Between these opposites, too, French life and thought have been torn for more than a century. Nor is what they have in common any less significant. Personal devotion to family-life,[1] a readiness to cling unto death to the choice that has once been made and to accept the consequences of that choice with courage: in these characteristics, too, the man of the countryside and the man of the towns share something that is characteristic of France as a whole. It explains the strength of centrifugal, disruptive and individual forces in French life which are at once a source of weakness and of resilience. It produces a bias of mind which is in one aspect anarchical, in another tyrannical: and anarchy and tyranny, as the course of French history has shown, are not opposites but are mutually generating. It is democracy which is the opposite of both, and the recurrent weakness of democracy in France is that it has been the product of a parallelogram of forces, one side of which pointed towards anarchy, the other in the direction of despotism.

It is on the subterranean working of these forces, and on the nature of these latent trends in French life

[1]Laval remained always devoted to his wife and daughter; de Gaulle to his wife and four children.

and politics, that we may find some light thrown by the joint examination of the lives of these two men. They are men whom only France could have produced. Both wrestled with the greatest problems of their age. Biographically they are interesting because they are two important men. Historically they are interesting because they are two Frenchmen.

INDEX

INDEX

INDEX